Grime Fighters

Grime Fighters

How to Banish Dirt, Grime, and Germs from Your Home

Foolproof, Practical Strategies

The 20 Best Tools for Cleaning

The Most Effective Cleaning Materials

BARNES
&NOBLE
BOOKS
NEW YORK

Notice

The information in this book has been carefully researched, and all efforts have been made to ensure accuracy. Rodale Inc. assumes no responsibility for any injuries suffered or damages or losses incurred during or as a result of following this information. All information should be carefully studied and clearly understood before taking any action based on the information or advice in this book.

Material in this book appeared previously in *Clean It Fast, Clean It Right* (Rodale Inc., 1998)

This edition published by Barnes & Noble, Inc., by arrangement with Rodale Inc.

Printed in the United States of America
Rodale Inc. makes every effort to use acid-free ∞, recycled paper ♻.

"Formulas for a Clean Home and a Clean Planet" on page 26 is adapted from *Clean and Green* by Annie Berthold-Bond, ©1990 by Annie Berthold-Bond. Reprinted by permission of Ceres Press.

Cover Designer: Scott Protchko
Interior Designer: Tara Long
Cover Photographer: Kurt Wilson

ISBN 0–7607–3075–X

2 4 6 8 10 9 7 5 3 1   hardcover

Contents

Introduction

It's one of the hard facts of life: As much as we all enjoy living in a sparkling clean house, there are few of us who find pleasure in putting it into that condition. Cleaning just seems to take too much time and too much effort—or so we think.

Want to know the truth? Cleaning your house can be simple and quick—if you use a few smart strategies and the right tools. That's where this book can help.

In just 90 or so pages, *Grime Fighters* will show you everything you need to know to banish dirt, grime, and germs from your home. You'll discover the most efficient ways to clean each room—even tough spots like the kitchen and bathroom. You'll also see which cleaning materials work best in which situations—and which could harm you if you don't use them properly.

Along the way, this book will teach you a few little-known facts about cleaning, too. For instance, did you know that:

▸ The green tarnish that forms inside a copper pot is more than just an eye-sore? (It's toxic—get rid of it!)

▸ A spritz of hairspray can wipe an ink stain off your favorite shirt?

▸ Simply shutting the toilet lid when you flush can dramatically reduce the amount of bacteria in your bathroom?

▸ You can make an inexpensive poultice out of baking soda that will draw stubborn stains out of china or porcelain?

Yes, *Grime Fighters* is filled with clever advice that will save you time, effort, and money. But most of all, this book will help you get control over household cleaning. Armed with the advice in this book, you can speed through your home when it gets dirty, and keep it neater and cleaner in between.

Cleaning doesn't have to be drudgery. With just a little effort, you can have a home that's pleasant to live in and healthier for you, too.

Let *Grime Fighters* show you how.

Clean Living

Get into a Clean Mindset

A Look at the Bright Side: You'll Save Time and Money—And Feel Better, Too

For Snow White, cleaning came easily. Not only did she have an army of cute little forest creatures to help her sanitize the Seven Dwarves' home but also she knew how to clean the house with a smile on her face and a hop in her step. Her secret? Whistling while she worked.

So much for fairy tales. If we could just pucker up and blow our cares away, we would all be whistling virtuosos. In the real world, cleaning is just not the kind of subject that gets people tapping toes or turning pirouettes.

Still, cleaning around the house is a vital part of daily existence, a practice that provides many rewards—not the least of which are more pleasant surroundings and better health. Who wouldn't want a home that's clean and clutter-free and stays that way with minimum effort?

You can have that. But achieving it starts with a positive mindset and some basic motivation skills for both you and your family. Master the advice in this chapter, and you'll be well on your way. You'll realize that keeping your home clean is not such a daunting task after all. And *that* would be something to whistle about.

Why Bother with Cleaning at All?

Could it be that we scour, mop, and vacuum our lives away for no good reason? After all, fad and fashion have pushed upon us such tortures as bustles and spike heels for no practical reason. Maybe you and your home would manage fine with the grunge look if you could just weather a little disapproval from a few family members and friends.

The truth is that cleaning has four major benefits. Let's examine each to show you the value of clean living.

Cleaning Saves Money

You know that brushing your teeth can save you thousands of dollars in dental bills. Well, the same thinking applies to all the things you own. Dirty stuff wears out faster than clean stuff. Simple preventive practices, including cleaning, can extend the life of everything from appliances to upholstery and, in turn, spare your pocketbook.

Moreover, regular cleaning makes for easier, less risky cleaning. Regular cleaning is more gentle to household surfaces. It minimizes the need for scrubbing, which causes wear and tear on walls, floors, and furniture.

Cleaning Saves Time

What could save more time than just avoiding the drudgery of cleaning altogether?

By keeping on top of dirt and clutter, you save time and effort. Wipe up a spill on your stove top before dinner and it takes you seconds to clean. Put it off until later and it becomes a dried-up mess that requires more time, more effort, and more cleaning products to remove, says Carol Seelaus, a speed-cleaning instructor at Temple University in Philadelphia and owner of Somebody's Gotta Do It, a professional cleaning service.

Cleaning Protects Your Health

A dirty house can make you sick. Whether it's an allergy to the thriving colony of dust mites that reside in your mattress or a case of food poisoning, the risk of illness from exposure to germs in the home is real. An estimated 50 to 80 percent of food-borne illnesses originate in the home, says Charles Gerba, Ph.D., professor of microbiology at the University of Arizona in Tucson. "People think that they have 'the 24-hour bug.' Well, the truth is that there's no such thing. It's usually food-borne or water poisoning," Dr. Gerba says.

Hot zones around the house that need regular disinfecting include sinks, faucets, doorknobs, cutting boards, the refrigerator handle, and the toilets.

Cleanliness Is Comforting

Cleaning makes things look good and makes us feel good. Forget about company coming. The main reason that people clean, according to a 1996 survey conducted by the Soap and Detergent Association in New York City, is to feel good about themselves.

"I call it house pride," says Seelaus. "The house is an extension of oneself, and if it looks good, it's a good reflection on oneself."

Now Slide into a Routine

Are you motivated to clean now? Don't start just yet—randomly attacking the house won't lead to long-term success. Experts agree that you need a regular cleaning routine. With a systematic approach, you assign the basic cleaning duties to a daily, weekly, monthly, or seasonal schedule—a move that will free you from the burdens of domestic chaos. A cleaning schedule saves time, effort, and frustration.

Look at it this way: You wouldn't think of going on vacation without knowing where you're going and how to get there. So when it comes to planning your housework, think of cleanliness as your destination and your cleaning schedule as the route you follow.

"With housework, the shortest distance between two points—starting and finishing—is a housekeeping schedule," says Deniece Schofield, a home management consultant in Cedar Rapids, Iowa, and author of *Confessions of an Organized Homemaker*. If you're domestically challenged, a schedule puts necessary tasks in writing so that the dirt and clutter do not overwhelm you. If you're a perfectionist, a schedule will keep you from doing tasks more often than they need to be done.

"I think that schedules are so important because housework is never done. But schedules make it feel done. That feeling of accomplishment, of being finished, is vital to housework," says Schofield. And don't worry that you'll have to consult your cleaning schedule every day for the rest of your life. The good habits you develop from following a schedule will soon become routine.

Four Steps to Bringing Order to Chaos

There is no magic formula that works for each and every household. Make a schedule that works for you by following these steps:

1. Decide how much time will be spent cleaning. On how many days of the week will you schedule cleaning time? How many hours each day? The number of hours you plan to devote to cleaning (and maintaining) will provide the rough framework for your schedule

2. For each room or area in your house, make a list of the jobs that need to be done. Include day-to-day jobs such as picking up, dusting, and vacuuming as well as once-a-year jobs like cleaning under furniture or appliances.

3. Next to each task, write down how often each job needs to be done—daily, weekly, monthly, or seasonally. How often you clean will depend

HOW TO CLEAN LIKE A PRO

People are often amazed by how much a housekeeper can accomplish in 4 hours, says Margaret Dasso, owner of the Clean Sweep, a professional cleaning service based in Lafayette, California, and coauthor of *Dirt Busters*. You can spend less time cleaning if you approach it the way a professional housecleaner does. "The more nearly you can duplicate these conditions, the more you will accomplish during your own cleaning time," she says.

Work from a list—and prioritize. A professional has a clear idea of what needs to be done. Make a list for yourself of what you will accomplish during your cleaning. Add a list of extra chores to be done if time and energy permit. Then stick to the list. If you see something else that needs to be done, make a mental note and schedule it for another day. "Distraction is your number one enemy when cleaning your own home," says Dasso.

Get the kids out of the house for a few hours. A professional does not have to deal with people underfoot. If possible, clean when there is no one else around. You won't have the distraction of trying to do two jobs at once.

Don't answer the telephone. "Every break in your routine is a time robber," says Dasso. "Interruptions are far more time-consuming than they seem." Take the phone off the hook or let the answering machine pick up.

Straighten up before you clean. A professional comes into a house that's ready to be cleaned. Get your house ready by picking up clutter the night before.

Set a time limit. Professionals are usually paid by the hour and must work within a certain time frame. Setting a time limit for yourself will keep you moving and on track.

Reward yourself for a job well-done. Professionals are paid for their work. Since no one is going to pay you to clean your own house, doing something nice for yourself does wonders for your motivation. "Whether it's a banana split, a great book, or a leisurely bubble bath, give yourself a treat," says Dasso.

upon the conditions in your house. A bathroom used by several people may need daily cleaning, for instance, while a single person with two bathrooms may clean only once a week. Daily vacuuming might seem excessive to some people and necessary to others.

4. Decide who will be responsible for each job. Post the schedule in a form you are comfortable with—in poster form or on index cards, for example. Until you memorize your routine, you will probably need to consult the schedule frequently.

It's All in the Timing

Here's an example of what your schedule might look like:

Daily: Straighten up, do all dishes, wipe stove and countertops, make beds, hang up clothes, read and dispose of mail, and clean up any spots and spills.

Weekly: Vacuum carpets, sweep and mop floors, dust furniture, change beds, clean bathrooms, spot-clean handprints, and empty all trash cans.

Monthly: Dust along woodwork, vacuum upholstery and window treatments, wipe kitchen cabinets, clean out refrigerator, and sweep garage.

Seasonally (twice a year—at the end of summer and winter): Defrost freezer, wash windows and walls, clean chimney, oven, furnace filters, light fixtures, and window blinds.

Hone Your Cleaning Smarts
How to Get More Sparkle in Less Time with Less Effort

Nobody misses June Cleaver. A lot has changed since the days when the domestic ideal meant cleaning an already-immaculate house in your pumps and pearls. A pristine home is still important to many Americans today. But according to a 1997 survey by the Soap and Detergent Association in New York City, almost 40 percent of us say that it's tough to find the time or energy to keep our homes clean.

Still, no matter how finicky or nonchalant you may be about housekeeping, the prospect of getting it done with a minimum amount of time and effort is alluring indeed. Here's a look at strategies for thorough-but-fast cleaning, and a guide to calling in the reinforcements—professional cleaners—for the really tricky jobs.

Room-by-Room Strategies

When you're ready to actually get some cleaning done—to apply a dust cloth to that vase and a mop to your linoleum—a few simple guidelines will ensure that you're working efficiently:

▶ Avoid distractions. Don't get sidetracked by lugging Junior's skates to his closet or stray socks to the laundry room.

▶ Work your way around the room in an orderly progression. Zipping from one side of the room to another again and again will waste a lot of footwork.

▶ Take all your cleaning tools with you. You waste time when you frequently stop your work to get more tools from the pantry or basement. And if you work without all the tools you need, you may be tempted to skip tasks that need attention.

Here's how to apply those principles as you go about your regular house-cleaning for both general living areas, like living rooms and bedrooms, and those two notorious hot spots, kitchens and bathrooms.

Make like a Hotel Housekeeper

The key to cleaning a room fast and efficiently is staying in the room until the cleaning is done, says Deniece Schofield, a home management consultant in Cedar Rapids, Iowa, and author of *Confessions of an Organized Homemaker*. One way to accomplish that is by using a utility cart that you can purchase at janitorial supply stores. They cost anywhere from $180 to $230. Like professional housekeepers in hotels, Schofield wheels her cart from room to room as she cleans. The top of the cart holds a tray with cleaning supplies and cloths. A garbage bag hangs from one side of the cart. A second bag or a pillowcase hangs on the other side of the cart to carry misplaced articles picked up from the room.

HEY, WHAT DO I CLEAN FIRST?

Here's an easy-to-remember strategy that will save you loads of grief as you clean a room: Start with the "dry" methods first. Always do as much vacuuming, sweeping, scraping, or dusting as possible before you douse something with water or spray it with cleaner. You wouldn't think of throwing a plate in the dishwasher if half of your dinner was still stuck to it. You would scrape it off first. The same idea applies to the surfaces in your home. Remove the bulk of the mess without getting it wet.

Then, when it's time to wield the sprays, sponges, and wet mops, here are a few more basic points to remember. First, wet the thing you're cleaning with the appropriate cleaning solution. Then, be patient—let the cleaner do its work. Save yourself some elbow grease and give the cleaner time to loosen and dissolve the dirt. Vigorous scrubbing not only takes a lot of energy but also can damage some surfaces.

Once the cleaning solution has done its work, it should be easy to wipe the dirt away, using a sponge, cloth, paper towel, or squeegee.

Here's how she recommends you work a room: Wheel the cart in. Remove the caddy of cleaning supplies and place all the soiled laundry in the cart. Put all the trash from the room in the garbage bag attached to the cart. Any misplaced items that do not belong in the room should be placed in the second bag. Now clean the room, working your way around the room in a circular fashion. As a general rule, start at the top and work your way down. The floor should be the last thing you do.

If buying a utility cart sounds like too big a step, Schofield suggests that you test the method first. The same technique can be accomplished with a garbage bag and a laundry basket. Use a caddy for your cleaning supplies and cloths. Instead of the cart, place all the soiled laundry in the basket and garbage in the bag. Place any misplaced items outside the door of each room. After you've emptied the laundry basket, use it to tote the articles that need to be put away.

A Pro's Recipe for the Kitchen

The kitchen is one of the two biggest cleaning tasks in any house (the other is the bathroom). To get through it quickly, Margaret Dasso, owner of the Clean Sweep, a professional cleaning service based in Lafayette, California, and coauthor of *Dirt Busters*, recommends the following strategies:

▸ If you have an electric stove with drip pans, remove them (when the burners are cool) and put them in a strong solution of automatic dishwasher detergent in the sink.

▸ Check floors, counters, and cabinets for any stubborn spots, such as dried-on food. Spray them with all-purpose cleaner and let them soak.

▸ Clean the spill tray underneath the stove burners by lifting the burners and reaching with a cloth or sponge into the holes where the drip pans were, or lifting up the stove top. Polish the stove top, knobs (make sure that you don't accidentally turn them on), and backsplash with all-purpose cleaner or glass cleaner.

▸ Scour the drip pans that have been soaking with a nylon scrubber or plastic brush. Dry them and place them back in the stove.

▸ Move to your left or right around the room in an orderly manner. Carry your supplies with you so that you do not have to retrace your steps.

▸ Polish appliance surfaces with glass cleaner and paper towels. Wipe doors on the inside and outside.

- As you go, clean and polish countertops. Pull items forward, clean behind them, and then slide them back. Check cabinets for fingerprints and clean them off with an all-purpose cleaner.
- If you have a windowsill above the sink, wash it.
- Clean the sink. Use an old toothbrush around the garbage disposal opening and the lip around the edge of the sink.
- Polish sink fixtures. Use a toothbrush around handles and the base of the fixture.
- Empty the trash.
- Sweep or vacuum the floor.
- Mop the floor.

Now Plunge into the Bathroom

In the same vein, here are Dasso's suggested strategies for tackling the bathroom:

- Remove throw rugs.
- Sweep or vacuum hair from the counter, sink, and floor. Use a wet paper towel instead of a sponge and save yourself the effort of cleaning the hair off the sponge.
- Spray the bathtub, shower walls, tile, and shower doors or curtain with an all-purpose cleaner.
- Clean the soap dish and any chrome fixtures in the shower.
- Spray a small amount of glass cleaner on the mirror. To avoid streaks, wipe until it is completely dry.
- Spray the sink and counter with all-purpose cleaner and wipe them dry. Move vanity items to one side, clean the vanity, and then slide them back.
- Clean the toilet, bowl first. Flush. Put the toilet seat up and spray and wipe each side with disinfectant cleaner. Clean the tank, base, handle, and any exposed pipes.
- Wipe the toilet paper holder.
- Go around the perimeter of the room. Wipe towel racks, refold towels, and dust the pictures and shelves. Check for fingerprints on doors and light switches, and clean with an all-purpose spray cleaner. To avoid shock, don't spray the light switches directly—spray your cleaning cloth first, then wipe.
- Wash the floor and replace rugs after it dries.

Make a Clean Break from Messy Habits

Little changes to your daily routine can speed up your cleaning by preventing your house from getting dirty in the first place. "Everyone is time-constrained or energy-constrained when it comes to cleaning," says cleaning consultant Kent Gerard from Oakland, California. "Through daily habits that don't generate filth in the first place, you can keep your house cleaner."

A few seconds or minutes of preventive maintenance can add up to hours of time saved on cleaning day.

11 Preventive Practices

Cleaning experts recommend that you build these 11 practices into your everyday routine. They'll make cleaning day in your home much easier and will help keep bacteria at bay.

1. **Ventilate the bathroom.** Excess moisture left in the air after bathing or showering promotes the growth of mildew, mold, and fungus. If you have a ventilation fan, use it. If not, open the bathroom window for a few minutes. If you don't have a window or a fan in the bathroom, try opening the window in a nearby room.

2. **Close the toilet seat when you flush.** Studies from the department of microbiology at the University of Arizona in Tucson show that when you flush, a mist is propelled from the toilet. The microscopic, bacteria-laden water droplets contaminate surfaces in the bathroom, creating the potential for infection.

3. **Squeegee the shower walls after use.** "It takes a minute and a half, and makes your weekly bathroom cleaning a 15-minute job," says Carol Seelaus, a speed-cleaning instructor at Temple University in Philadelphia and owner of Somebody's Gotta Do It, a professional cleaning service. The three major cleaning problems in bathtubs and showers—soap scum, mildew, and mineral buildup—are caused by allowing water to stand until it evaporates. By drying the walls right away, you prevent all three problems.

   "A lot of people have a problem with using a squeegee," says Seelaus. "They ask, 'Can't I just dry it with a towel?' The answer is yes, but then you have a soaking wet towel to deal with." One shortcut she recommends is to use liquid soap products instead of bar soaps when bathing. They don't contain the fat that causes soap scum to form.

4. **Ban stove-top splatter art.** In the kitchen, use bigger pots and pans when cooking. When *Woman's Day* magazine surveyed 1,000 women

THE BASICS OF EFFICIENT CLEANING

To keep yourself sane and to make maximum use of your cleaning time, cleaning pros recommend that you follow these guidelines:

1. Keep your cleaning supplies together. Before you start, gather your equipment and cleaning products and load them in a tray, apron, or bucket. You won't waste time running from room to room for supplies.

If it's not dirty, don't clean it. Don't waste time and energy sanitizing an unused bathroom just because it's cleaning day.

3. Spot-clean whenever possible. Don't clean the entire oven when only the glass door has a grease mark.

4. Don't scrub. Let the cleaning solution do the work for you. Spray tough spots—like a soap-scummed shower wall—with cleaner and let it soak while you clean something else. This way you'll make double use of your time and save elbow grease.

5. Less is more. Use only as much cleaning product as you need. Using too much is a waste of money, and it means more time is spent mopping up the excess.

to find out the household chores that they absolutely hate, cleaning the stove came up as number one.

"A lot of spills and boil-overs are caused by cooking with too small a pan. People say, 'I don't want to wash a big pot,' and then they wind up having to wash the whole stove," says Seelaus.

5. Blow grease and odors away. Use an exhaust fan while you're cooking and you'll eliminate airborne grease that builds up on kitchen surfaces. You'll also reduce cooking odors, which can be absorbed by carpets and upholstery.

6. Don't let germs hitchhike. Use a clean sponge or dishcloth to mop up messes and spills. Everything from countertops to cabinets to refrigerator handles can be blanketed in a coating of thriving bacteria after a swipe with a germ-laden sponge or dishcloth. Moist cellulose sponges provide just the right environment for colony-forming microbes—a

surface to cling to, moisture, and a steady supply of nutrients. The same holds true for cotton dishcloths.

"From a microbial standpoint, the cleanest people actually have the dirtiest kitchens because they are always wiping everything down," says Charles Gerba, Ph.D., professor of microbiology at the University of Arizona in Tucson.

7. Empty the dishwasher promptly. If the dishwasher is full of clean dishes, no one can load it with dirty dishes. So the dirty dishes end up in the kitchen sink, creating a mess that has to be cleaned up prior to meal preparation instead of after.

8. Put a mat at each entrance to your home. About 80 percent of the dirt on floors comes in through the door, says Seelaus. If you stop dirt from being tracked in by wiping it off or better yet, removing your shoes, you'll have cleaner floors and carpets.

   Avoid decorative mats, carpet squares, and link mats made of old tires. Instead, purchase a commercial mat from a restaurant supply store or janitorial supply store. They come in various sizes and range in price from $12 to $37. An effective mat can reduce the cleaning time in the average household by 200 hours per year.

9. Shut dirt out. Keep drawers, cabinets, closets, and furniture closed. In the kitchen, food and crumbs won't end up inside a closed silverware drawer. Dust has a way of infiltrating everything, but items stored away in closets will stay clean longer if the doors are shut.

10. Put things back where they belong. Clutter is the number one cleaning problem in most homes—about half of the housework is caused by junk that's lying around. When clogged with the clutter of carelessly strewn objects, no room can be cleaned fast or efficiently. You waste time and energy picking up each object, deciding where it's supposed to be, and putting it away. Altering this habit is probably the most difficult because clutter is an ongoing battle.

11. Provide plenty of litter receptacles. Another way to avoid clutter is to make sure that there is always a readily available place to throw things away.

Calling in the Reinforcements

The soap scum in your shower is so thick you can write your name in it. And your in-laws are on their way for their annual visit. Uh-oh.

You might be one of the nearly 10 million Americans each year who decide to pay professionals to clean their homes. Although homes with children under age 18 may need the most cleaning help, the people most likely to hire such help are empty-nesters—age 45-plus. Here's how to hire the right pro for the right job.

Choose the Right Helper

If you're looking for a housecleaning service, there are two basic routes to take: Hire a housekeeper, or hire a professional cleaning service. There are a number of factors to consider, says Dasso—cost, reliability, frequency of use, convenience, and the type of cleaning to be done.

The cost of hiring a cleaning person, or housekeeper, can vary from $5 an hour for a college student to more than $12 an hour for a trained professional. In addition to cleaning, housekeepers will often perform tasks such as babysitting, folding and putting away laundry, and picking up clutter. If you need this kind of flexibility and personal service, hiring a housekeeper is a good solution, says Dasso.

Professional cleaning services descend on a home with one or more cleaners and whip the place into shape. They are usually hired to do a predetermined, standardized cleaning and are in and out of your home in a very short amount of time, Dasso says. The cost is usually $50 to $85 per visit.

Because their services are strictly cleaning, you'll need to pick up and have things out of the way when professional cleaning services come. If you don't need regular help but have a special event coming up, such as a party, or if you just want to get the spring cleaning out of the way, professional services are a good choice.

When you hire a professional housecleaner, be sure that you both understand the services that will be provided—what is going to be cleaned, how long it will take, how much it will cost, and how frequently it will be done.

Put Dry Cleaners to the Test

Dry cleaning is called dry only because clothes are washed in solvents instead of water. Fabrics that can be harmed by contact with water, such as silk or wool, are laundered in a mixture of solvents, soap, and a tiny bit of water in big front-loading washing machines. Remember: The chemical cleaning process is hard on fibers, and frequent cleaning can cause some fabrics, such as wool, to develop a sheen, according to Jennifer Morgan, Ph.D., product technologist for the Wool Bureau in New York City.

Clothing does not need to be dry-cleaned every time it is worn. After wearing, brush the garment off or shake it out to remove surface soils, then let it air out. Inspect the garment for any spills or stains. If the fabric is visibly soiled, take it to the cleaners. Whenever possible, tell the dry cleaner the source of stains and spots—they'll be able to do a better job for you, says Dr. Morgan.

Your clothes should come back from the cleaners looking like new. But that doesn't always happen. If you're shopping for a new cleaner, dry-cleaning experts suggest that you try this test: Pick two garments that you're not too fond of, one in a bright color and the other white. Give them to the prospective cleaner and see how they come back. Ask yourself the following questions, suggests Jerry Levine, associate director of the Neighborhood Cleaners Association International in New York City.

▶ Does the color look the same as when you sent it? Is the white clean or dingy looking? Some dry cleaners try to cut corners by not purifying the solvents often enough to remove dissolved stain material. Or they might not replace or regenerate the filters in their machines frequently enough, leaving solids in the solvent that could damage your clothing.

▶ Where are the tags attached? Garments need to be identified so they do not get lost. The tags, however, should never be stapled to the garment itself, but to the label. Some finer dry cleaners will remove the tags from the garment and attach them to the invoice.

▶ Did they touch up the ironing, or just machine press it? The cleaner should touch up garments that have special darts or pleats, like a fitted blouse or a pleated skirt, with a hand iron to remove any creases left by the pressing machine. Some try to save on labor costs by skipping this step.

▶ Are all the stains that can be removed gone? Stains should be taken out by hand. The more training the cleaner has, the more likely that stains will be removed.

▶ Are all buttons still on the garment? Are any damaged? Some buttons are solvent-soluble. A good dry cleaner should take care to protect buttons from solvents or should recommend removing them before cleaning.

"And remember," says Levine, "don't expect the best quality cleaning for the lowest price. They don't go together. Cheap usually means a lousy cleaner."

For Drapes, Carpets, and Upholstery, Turn Up the Heat

There's actually no steam involved in professional steam cleaning. Dirt and soils are removed from draperies, carpets, and upholstery through a process of hot-water extraction. Special machinery applies a cleaning solution and then suctions the soiled water from the fibers. Although you can rent this type of machine at rental centers and grocery stores for less than $40 a day (cleaning solutions are extra), they usually do not remove water as effectively as professional machinery.

And if you don't remove it, you'll be the one in hot water. "Damage occurs when fibers stay wet for too long," says Claudia Ramirez, former executive vice president of the Association of Specialists in Cleaning and Restoration (ASCR) in Millersville, Maryland. The longer the fabric is wet, the more likely you are to get dye bleeding, odors, and mildew. "Mildew can start forming in just 24 hours," she says.

Under normal use, carpet should be cleaned once a year, and draperies and upholstery every 2 years, says Ramirez. You may have to clean them more often if you have a smoker, young children, or pets in the home, or if you live in a region with high humidity, extreme cold, or excessive airborne dust.

Here are tips for working with a steam cleaner:

Check out the training. You want a steam-cleaning service that is adequately trained, so contact the Carpet and Upholstery Cleaning Institute at the Association of Specialists in Cleaning and Restoration, 8229 Cloverleaf Drive, Suite 460, Millersville, MD 21108. Ask for a free list of professional carpet and upholstery cleaners in your region. Members of ASCR are backed by technical advisors and the organization's laboratory if a cleaning problem comes up.

Walk and talk. Do a walk-through inspection with the contractor. "This is your time to point out any special areas of concern," says Ramirez. "This way, everyone is aware of the expectations."

Watch for the preliminaries. A steam-cleaning contractor should not just enter your house and start cleaning the carpet or upholstery right away. A professional will avoid costly mistakes by inspecting and testing fabrics first.

When Your Ducts Go South

The heating and air-conditioning systems in your home have filters that will trap most dust, pet dander, and other particles and keep them out of your duct system. If you clean or change the filter regularly, your ducts should stay reasonably clean.

You may need professional duct cleaning, however, if you've had an unusually high level of contamination in your house—say, remodeling that created large amounts of dust, a furnace malfunction that forced soot into the

DESIGN DIRT OUT OF YOUR LIFE

Dirt happens—you can't totally banish it from your life. But you can reduce the amount of time it takes to clean your home by choosing low-maintenance materials when you buy items such as furniture, fixtures, flooring, and carpeting.

An example is a light-colored floor that requires an extra half-hour of sweeping and mopping each week; it will cost you 26 hours of time in the course of a year. Now, that floor is likely to last 10 years, so you'll spend 10 days more cleaning it than you would if you had chosen a darker floor.

Here are some other ways that cleaning professionals say you can design dirt out of your life:

Keep it simple. The more fussy and ornate something is, the more difficult it is to clean, says Carol Seelaus, a speed-cleaning instructor at Temple University in Philadelphia and owner of Somebody's Gotta Do It, a professional cleaning service. Why spend hours working the dirt out of cracks and crevices when a sleek, simple design will do the job? Use the simplicity rule on everything from draperies to faucets.

Go for less surface. Look at design in terms of surface area. Every surface collects dust and dirt and requires cleaning. A louvered surface, like shutter doors, will be much more difficult to clean than a flat surface. Eliminate edges and ledges and textures and grooves. Each is a surface requiring another swipe of the cleaning cloth, so stick with smooth surfaces, Seelaus says.

Camouflage dirt. The idea isn't to wallow in hidden filth but to pick patterns and colors that blend with your lifestyle. If every strand of your dog's white hair shows on your dark blue carpeting, then you'll need to vacuum every day. A lighter color will camouflage the hair so you can stick to a reasonable cleaning routine. Patterns and designs will hide dirt and wear and tear because the eye is distracted. Solid colors, on the other hand, hide very little, cleaning professionals note. Select colors based on the number of kids you have, the color of your pets, or the color of your local soil.

system, or water damage. Moisture in ducts will promote the growth of mold, mildew, and bacteria. A professional duct cleaner will attach a vacuum device to your vents to suck out the dust and particles. The procedure is usually priced according to the number of vents in your home.

To make sure that you're hiring a competent duct cleaner, follow these tips from the ASCR:

Look for certification. Hire a certified mechanical hygienist (CMH), the highest recognition of competency in the duct-cleaning industry. Contractors who have earned a CMH designation are members of the Mechanical Systems Hygiene Institute, a division of the ASCR. They get ongoing technical updates, continuing accreditation in the latest cleaning techniques, and access to a network of technical advisors at ASCR. To find a CMH in your region, contact the ASCR at the address mentioned above for a free referral.

Expect an inspection. The first thing a duct-cleaning contractor should do is inspect the system visually and provide an assessment of what needs to be done.

For tough jobs only, seal it. Ideally, you want the dirt removed from your duct system. But sometimes contractors will recommend coating the interior of a duct with sealant to reline the system. The sealant is sprayed into the duct on top of existing dirt and dries to a lacquerlike finish to prevent dust from circulating. This may be necessary in hard-to-reach areas, but the contractor should remove as much dirt buildup as possible before resorting to sealants.

Give your ducts a checkup. To ensure that it is operating efficiently, have your ventilation system inspected annually by a member of the Mechanical Systems Hygiene Institute or by a heating, ventilation, and air-conditioning contractor. Dirt collects in areas where the air moves sluggishly. On air-conditioning systems, clean the condensation drip pan at the base of the unit regularly to prevent growth of molds and fungi. To do this, remove the drip pan from the unit, drain the excess water, and wash it with a sponge or cloth in a mild soap-and-water solution.

A Clean Bill of Health

Make Your Home and Your Planet Safer with Some Sanitation Savvy

You're sick of cleaning, you say? Just think how sick you would be without it. Each year, millions of people develop health problems because of improper or insufficient cleaning. Consider these facts:

▸ About 20 percent of the yearly 6.5 million cases of food-borne illness originate in the home when hands, utensils, and surfaces are contaminated by bacteria.

▸ About one in six Americans will be affected by an allergy-related illness sometime in his life.

▸ Between 1982 and 1994, the prevalence of asthma in the United States increased by 61.2 percent. Among children under age 18, the rate rose 72.3 percent.

Our comfortable homes with their wall-to-wall carpeting and weathertight insulation are the ideal places for allergens, such as dust mites, to live and multiply. If you suffer from allergies, no doubt you've been told to keep your home as clean as possible.

While a clean home may be healthier than a neglected one, the very cleaners that we use to sanitize and sparkle can be hazardous to our health. Cleaning exposes us to harsh chemical compounds that are as hard on humans as they are on the environment. Prolonged contact with many everyday cleaners like liquid household bleach can cause eye and skin irritation, respiratory tract irritation, nausea, and dizziness. Because most cleaners are marketed as friendly, helpful products designed to make our lives easier, it's easy to forget that safety hazards can also come in those perky little packages.

How to Hunt Microbes

The dirt detection capabilities of a white glove may be perfectly adequate for your coffee table, but in the kitchen and bathroom, unless you have a microscope, there's no way to see if it's clean enough. Dirt that you can't see—germs and bacteria—can make you sick by contaminating food, surfaces, and utensils.

The kitchen is the most germ-laden room in the house. Billions and billions of microbes from raw meat juices, festering dishcloths and sponges, rotting garbage, spoiled food, dirty dishes, and unwashed hands are found on every surface. From a health standpoint, a freshly wiped countertop may be the dirtiest place in your home.

"Clean people are usually the dirtiest because they spread the germs all around. The bachelor who never cleans is usually the cleanest from a germ standpoint," says Charles Gerba, Ph.D., professor of microbiology at the University of Arizona in Tucson.

Arm Yourself with Disinfectant

It's impossible to rid your surroundings of every microbial life form. Your goal shouldn't be to create a sterile environment but to exercise day-to-day cleanliness habits that discourage the growth of germs and bacteria, says Dr. Gerba.

Use a disinfectant cleaner approved for use in the kitchen for your routine kitchen cleaning and for daily cleanup on surfaces that have come in contact with raw meat. Most homemade cleaners, like concoctions made from vinegar or baking soda, or environmentally friendly cleaners have no disinfectant properties at all—they merely move germs around. To be sure that a product kills germs like salmonella, look for a disinfectant with an Environmental Protection Agency registration number on the label. Read the instructions. It may be necessary to leave the cleaner on the surface for a specified period of time in order to kill germs.

Although the bathroom has a reputation for being germ-infested, there are fewer microbes in it that are likely to make you sick than there are in the kitchen. This is probably because people tend to use disinfectants in their bathrooms more often than in their kitchens, Dr. Gerba says. Regular hand washing with soap and water is the best precaution against sickness or infection.

Six Germ-Stopping Habits

To keep microbes in check, follow these tips recommended by Dr. Gerba:

Rub-a-dub, bub. Wash your hands frequently. Your hands and fingers are common transmitters of germs and bacteria. The National Restaurant

Association's hand-washing recommendations include using warm soapy water for at least 20 seconds and rinsing thoroughly with clean water. Follow this procedure both before and after preparing foods (especially when you handle raw poultry, meat, or seafood), using the bathroom, and after sneezing, coughing, smoking, eating, or drinking. When washing your hands, the National Restaurant Association suggests that you pay particular attention to the areas underneath your fingernails and between your fingers.

Ditch your dishcloth. In a study of sponges and dishcloths, Dr. Gerba found that dishcloths are contaminated with more fecal coliform bacteria (an indicator of unsanitary conditions) than sponges.

Disinfect your sponge. Put your sponge in the dishwasher with the dishes daily. If it develops a pungent odor, discard it. Smell indicates the presence of germs. Sponges should be used for no longer than a month.

Do paperwork. Use paper towels to wipe up meat juices. Discard the towels and clean the surface with disinfectant cleaner.

Done eating? Get busy. Do your dishes right after meals. Bacteria thrive on unwashed dishes. While a dishwasher will sanitize your dishes and utensils, they don't stay that way. Make sure to wash your hands before you put them away to avoid contaminating the sanitized dishes.

Take it outside. Empty the trash every day. Moist, rotting garbage is a haven for germ growth, so make taking out the trash a nightly ritual. When preparing meat, make sure to dispose of the packaging promptly by wrapping it in plastic and putting it in the trash, says cleaning consultant Kent Gerard from Oakland, California. Letting it lie on the counter could spread germs.

Safe at Home

You've been using the same brand of all-purpose cleaner for years, so why would you need to read the label? Because it may be a different product without your knowing it: Product formulations change. To get an edge in the glutted market for household cleaners, manufacturers routinely reformulate their products to clean faster or clean better. New product ingredients may mean that additional precautions need to be taken with the product. So do read labels, even on your old favorites.

Remember that although they are user-friendly for the most part, household cleaners are chemical compounds that can be hazardous. And using them improperly can endanger your health or the environment, according to the U.S. Consumer Product Safety Commission (CPSC).

A cleaner is classified as hazardous if it displays one or more of these four properties:

Corrosive: Can dissolve or destroy living tissue or materials

Ignitable: Catches fire easily

Reactive: Can explode or react violently

Toxic: Can be poisonous or harmful when eaten, absorbed through the skin, or inhaled

Hazardous products are required by law to include a warning and description of the hazard on the label, says Wilma Hammett, Ph.D., professor and extension home furnishings specialist at the North Carolina Cooperative Extension Service at North Carolina State University in Raleigh. Words such as "danger," "warning," or "caution" will be printed on the label, indicating the level of the hazard. Here are the words you're likely to see and their definitions.

Caution: Moderately or slightly toxic

Warning: Moderately or slightly toxic

Poison: Highly toxic or poisonous

Danger: Extremely flammable, corrosive, or highly toxic

The product must also include a statement telling you how to avoid the hazard and how to use the product safely.

Heading Off Accidents

Here's how to handle cleaning products safely:

Keep the original. Always store household cleaning products in their original containers to avoid accidental misuse or poisoning, recommends the CPSC. Labels on the original packaging contain directions for use, safety precautions, and antidote or treatment information. Accidental swallowing is more likely to occur when cleaning products are placed in containers such as cups, soft drink bottles, and milk cartons, which children associate with food and drink. A brightly colored cleaner placed in such a container is a dangerous temptation.

Hide the bottles. Store cleaning compounds and all potentially hazardous household chemicals out of the reach of children and pets. More than 1 million children age 5 and under were exposed to potentially poisonous substances in 1995, according to the American Association of Poison Control Centers. Use locks or child-resistant latches to secure storage areas. On products that have child-resistant packaging, always resecure the child-resistant closure before putting it away.

Never mix cleaning products. Combining cleaning products can create hazardous fumes. The classic example is chlorine bleach and ammonia: When mixed together, they form a toxic gas that can cause loss of voice, coughing, a feeling of suffocation and burning, and possibly death. Some products, such as automatic dishwasher detergent and liquid cleansers, contain bleach and should not be mixed with ammonia-based products like window cleaners. Also, be careful when using toilet-bowl cleaners. Some contain acids, which can cause a dangerous reaction if mixed with other chemicals, according to the CPSC.

Go for the pump. Exposure to cleaning solutions, air fresheners, oven cleaners, and rug and upholstery cleaners can cause dizziness, nausea, and respiratory tract irritation. To reduce your exposure to potential irritants, use a pump spray instead of an aerosol whenever possible. The fine mist of aerosols is more easily inhaled.

Slow down. Hurrying and plain carelessness are frequently the cause of accidents in the home. According to the National Safety Council, accidental poisoning is second only to falls as the leading cause of death in the home. Take the time to do things the right way.

Here are a few more ways to protect yourself when using hazardous chemicals, says Dr. Hammett.

Stay under cover. Wear protective equipment, like rubber gloves, if recommended by the manufacturer.

Clear the air. Use products in a well-ventilated area. Open windows and use a fan to circulate the air. Take plenty of fresh-air breaks.

Don't work hand to mouth. Traces of chemicals can be carried from your hands to your mouth. So do not eat, drink, or smoke while using hazardous products.

Forget your contacts. Don't wear soft contact lenses when working with solvents and pesticides. Soft contacts can absorb and hold the chemical next to your eyes.

Keep a lid on it. Keep containers tightly closed between applications to avoid spills and make the contents less accessible to children.

Stay on guard. Do not leave products unattended while using them if there is a chance that a child could handle them.

Savvy Use of Solvents

Some household cleaners contain organic solvents—usually a petroleum product that is added to keep the product in its liquid or paste form or to enable it to dissolve dirt and grease. Products containing organic solvents evaporate readily and quickly fill a room with fumes. The fumes can cause intoxication, drowsiness, disorientation, and headaches. The CPSC requires that hazardous ingredients be identified on the label. Read the label; it's there for your safety.

Long-term exposure to some organic solvents, such as methylene chloride, which is found in some paint strippers, degreasers, and waxes, can damage the nervous system and may cause cancer in humans. For example, 1,1,1 trichlorethane, which is found in drain cleaners, spot removers, and shoe polish, can damage the nervous system.

Very high doses of cleaners containing petroleum distillates or organic solvents—furniture polish and spot remover are among a vast array of products—can lead to lung problems, an irregular heartbeat, and skin rashes.

Cut your risks when using organic solvents by taking these precautions, says the CPSC.

▸ Use solvents outdoors, if possible. If you must work indoors, open windows and doors and use a fan as you work. Wear a respirator (a mask that comes with special filter cartridges for different types of fumes—be sure that it's made from a material that cannot be permeated by the substance you are handling) and goggles, if necessary. If you decide to wear a respirator, check with your doctor first. You must have good lung function to operate the filter cartridges. And make sure that you get the proper filter and that the mask fits well.

▸ Don't use more than one solvent product at a time, and don't use one immediately after another.

▸ Fumes of some solvents tend to sink, so you may inhale more vapors if you are bent over while working.

▸ Alcoholic beverages can heighten the toxic effects of solvent fumes. Don't drink alcohol if you will be using a solvent that day.

▸ Many solvents are flammable, so use them away from heat or flames.

Getting Clean, Staying Green

Most households contain dozens of chemical products that have the potential to pollute our soil, air, and water, if used improperly or disposed of carelessly. The average American household generates about 15 pounds of hazardous waste each year and may have more than 100 pounds of it stored away at any one time.

Cleaners aren't the worst of the household polluters. They rank fourth, behind maintenance items like paint, batteries, and personal-care products such as hair spray and deodorant. But cleaners do account for more than 10 percent of all hazardous waste generated per year per household.

Many household cleaners, in the amounts normally used, can be safely washed down the drain if you are served by either a municipal sewer system or a septic system, says Robert Rubin, Ph.D., professor of biological and agricultural engineering at North Carolina State University in Raleigh. This applies to dishwashing and laundry products, bleaches, toilet-bowl cleaners,

FORMULAS FOR A CLEAN HOME AND A CLEAN PLANET

What good is having a clean home if it means polluting the planet? Here's how to make an Earth-friendly cleaning kit that's devoid of potentially harmful cleaners or toxic chemicals. You'll need just six readily available ingredients: baking soda, white vinegar, lemon juice, olive oil, salt, and borax.

From these common household items, you can make cleaners that are in many cases as effective as commercial products, but are safer and less costly. Here are a few formulas for homemade "green" cleaners.

Fabric softener. Add ¼ cup vinegar during the rinse cycle of your laundry. Clothes will feel softer and smell fresh.

Furniture polish. Mix 2 tablespoons olive oil and 1 tablespoon vinegar in 1 quart warm water. Store it in a spray bottle. (*Note:* This solution works best when kept warm. Let the bottle rest in a bucket of hot water while using.) Apply with a polishing cloth to produce a clean, shiny surface.

Glass cleaner. Mix ½ cup vinegar and 1 gallon warm water in a pump spray bottle.

Toilet-bowl cleaner. Pour 1 cup borax and ¼ cup vinegar or lemon juice into the bowl. Let it sit for 2 hours and then scour thoroughly with a brush.

Drain cleaner. Pour ½ cup baking soda down the drain. Add ¼ cup vinegar and ½ cup salt. Let it sit for 15 minutes (the mixture will bubble and gurgle noisily), then pour a kettle of boiling water down the drain. Be sure to cover your face and hands.

and all-purpose cleaners. But large quantities can overload either system to the point that its treatment does not meet specific water-quality standards when it is released into lakes, rivers, and streams.

Solvent Disposal: Get with a Program

For the most part, only organic solvent-based cleaning products such as spot removers, paint thinners, metal and furniture cleaners, drain cleaners, and degreasers are considered hazardous to the environment and fit the criteria mentioned above. Unfortunately, many make their way into sewage treatment plants, landfills, and incinerators when people dump them down the drain or simply throw them in the trash. This not only poses a threat to the environment but also can harm sanitation workers.

If you cannot recycle or reuse such a product, store it until you can dispose of it through household hazardous waste collection programs, which are periodically sponsored by many communities. Call your city or county environmental management or waste management division (listed in the government offices section of your phone book) for information.

The most common type of program is a collection day that offers residents a periodic opportunity to take wastes to a central location where they are sorted and then recycled or sent to an appropriate disposal site.

When you want to dispose of solvent-based materials, leave them sealed tightly in their original containers. Store them in a well-ventilated location, says Dr. Hammett. If they are flammable, store them away from sources of heat, sparks, or ignition. Be sure that they are not stored with or near corrosive products.

Reduce Your Chemical Dependence

Here are ways to reduce your use of chemical products.

Buy versatile cleaners. Contrary to what manufacturers want you to believe, you do not need a different product to clean each surface in your home, says Dr. Hammett. Multipurpose cleaners will reduce the number of hazardous cleaners in your home and save you money.

Take it easy. Buy the least harmful product available. Learn to identify hazardous products from their labels. Remember the difference between a product labeled "danger" and one that is labeled "caution."

To reduce the danger in your home and the impact on the environment, use cleaners labeled "warning" or "caution." And don't be fooled by the label "nontoxic." That's a marketing term that is not defined by the federal government, so it can be used on products that are indeed toxic.

Buy only what you need. To avoid the need to store or dispose of unused cleaners, buy the smallest amount needed to do the cleaning task.

Five Paths to Cleaning Conservation

You can be kind to our environment simply by using up fewer resources when you clean. Here are five ways to do that, according to cleaning expert Don Aslett in his book *The Cleaning Encyclopedia.*

1. Use concentrated cleaners. They use less packaging and are cheaper, too. Recycle your empties.

2. Clean with reusable products. Use cloths that you can launder when you're through, instead of disposable paper towels. (Be careful when disposing of cloths you have used with hazardous chemicals—read the manufacturer's label for disposal instructions.)

3. Don't put it off. More accumulated dirt means that more energy, cleaning supplies, and water will be needed to do the job.

4. Use energy efficiently. Use cold water when you can—when running the garbage disposal or washing floors, for instance. Make sure that you have a full load before you use the dishwasher, washer, or dryer. Make sure that all the clutter is picked up before you turn on the vacuum cleaner.

5. Use only what you need. Cleaners (like laundry detergent or floor cleaner) work best when they are mixed with a specific amount of water. Follow the instructions on the package carefully.

Combating Allergies

If you're one of the 50 million Americans who suffer from allergies, not only do you have to put up with the sneezing and itching but also you have to go the extra mile with cleaning routines, too. But the effort is worth it because specific cleaning procedures will reduce or eliminate the irritants from your home.

The most common allergy triggers are found in the home in house dust, which is made up of human skin particles, animal dander, and molds. Dust mites and cockroaches also produce allergic reactions. Symptoms, according to the American Academy of Allergy, Asthma, and Immunology, may include a blocked or runny nose with sneezing (especially in the morning), watery eyes, itchy rashes, coughing, and wheezing. Many people may not be aware that they have allergies and may only experience occasional symptoms.

What's Bugging You?

A doctor can determine what you're allergic to by taking a medical history and doing a series of skin tests. Here's a rundown of the most common household allergens.

Dust mites. Nearly 100,000 of these Lilliputian members of the spider family can live on a square yard of carpeting. The microscopic mites aren't the cause of the allergic reaction; their waste is. Dust mites dine on the skin cells that you shed every day. That's why they thrive wherever you spend the most time—beds, pillows, or your favorite stuffed chair. They produce about 20 tiny pellets of waste a day that contain a protein that many people are allergic to. Mites thrive in humid conditions, especially carpeting placed on a concrete floor.

Animal dander. It's a common misconception that people are allergic to the fur of an animal. The real cause of the problem is the protein in tiny flakes of pet skin and saliva that float through the air in the house, irritating your eyes, nose, and respiratory tract. Allergies to cats are the most common, but other animals can cause allergies as well.

Animal dander is light and remains airborne for a long time before falling to the floor. Vacuuming aggravates the condition by swirling allergens around the room. It may take over an hour for the dander to settle back down to the floor.

Mold. Mold thrives in moist areas of the house, such as bathrooms and basements. It's not the black grimy stuff growing on the tile grout that causes the allergic irritation but the reproductive spores it produces that are carried through the air.

Cockroaches. More than half of the people afflicted with allergies are allergic to cockroaches and their droppings. If you have cockroaches, they are normally evident in the kitchen.

Pollen. Pollen allergies are a seasonal problem, normally occurring in the spring and the fall when pollen invades your home through open doors and windows.

No More Sleeping with the Enemy

Ridding the house of a zillion microscopic particles seems like a daunting task, but some simple steps will greatly reduce your exposure. With allergic irritants lurking throughout the house, where do you start?

"The bedroom is where you spend the most time," says Gerard, who specializes in clients with allergies. "Where you spend the most time is where you want the least exposure to indoor pollutants."

AN ALLERGY-BUSTING SCHEDULE

If you have allergies to indoor pollutants like mold or dust mites, you probably have been told to keep your house as clean as possible. Supplement your regular cleaning schedule with the following tasks to keep allergens at bay, says Thomas Platts-Mills, M.D., Ph.D., head of the division of asthma, allergy, and immunology at the University of Virginia Health Sciences Center in Charlottesville and director of its Asthma and Allergic Disease Center.

Daily

▶ Ventilate the bathroom (using a fan, open window, or air-conditioning) to ensure that walls and curtains dry fully.

Weekly

▶ Wash all bedding—sheets, mattress pads, pillowcases, and bed covers—in hot water.

▶ Bathe pets in soap and water to loosen and remove dander.

▶ Before vacuuming, dust furniture, windowsills, and crevices with a slightly damp cloth.

Every 2 Weeks

▶ Vacuum plastic mattress, box spring, and pillow covers, then wipe with a slightly damp cloth.

Monthly

▶ Wash stuffed toys in hot water, or put them in the freezer in a plastic bag overnight to kill dust mites.

▶ Clean tubs, showers, and shower doors and curtains with a 10 percent solution of disinfectant or liquid household bleach and water (one part disinfectant or bleach and nine parts water) to kill molds. Scrub with a stiff-bristle brush and rinse with clean water. Wear gloves.

Here's how the American Academy of Allergy, Asthma, and Immunology recommends that you allergy-proof your bedroom:

▶ Keep the bedroom uncluttered and easy to clean. Avoid dust collectors such as books, knickknacks, stuffed animals, and televisions.

▶ Encase the mattress, box springs, and pillows in airtight, zippered plastic covers. Controlling dust mites in mattresses requires either regular vacuuming or keeping them in dust-free casings. Covering them is the easiest, most effective solution.

▶ Wash all bedding regularly in hot water—at least 130°F to kill dust mites. Comforters and pillows should be made of synthetic materials such as Dacron or Orlon so that they can be washed. Pillows should be washed regularly and replaced every 2 to 3 years.

These allergy-proofing tips apply not only to the bedroom but to the rest of the house as well:

▶ Remove carpeting, if possible. All types of allergens are abundant in carpeting. Replace it with hard flooring such as wood or vinyl.

▶ Keep the humidity low. To reduce the growth of dust mites and mold, keep the indoor relative humidity below 50 percent but above 30 percent. Central air-conditioning is the most effective way of controlling humidity. It cools and cleans indoor air and keeps outdoor air out. Dehumidifiers are useful in basements.

▶ Keep your pet off bedding and furniture. If he refuses to give up his favorite spot on the sofa, cover the area with a cloth that can be laundered frequently.

▶ Use the right vacuum. People with allergies should avoid vacuuming. While it cleans dust, it also stirs up dust. If you have to vacuum, wear a dust mask or use a vacuum with a HEPA (high-efficiency particulate air) or the newer ULPA (ultra low penetration air) filter. They're sold by allergy-supply and hospital-supply companies as well as discount stores and drugstores, and good ones can cost from $500 to $1,000. Avoid water vacs that filter dust into a canister of water. They can spew a fine mist of allergens.

Tools and Materials

Choosing Your Weapons

The Ultimate Primer on Cleaning Implements and Chemicals

The first half of this book provided strategies you can use to speed your housecleaning. Now it's time to talk about the second half of the equation: the tools and materials of cleaning. You'll need to know them well if you want to clean fast and do it right.

Most chores call only for the basics—things like an all-purpose cleaner, a white scrub pad, and a disinfectant. But occasionally, making a clean sweep of spills and stains requires slightly more exotic supplies such as spot removers, neat's-foot oil, or hydrogen peroxide.

Brushing up on the tools of the trade will save you money and ensure that you finish the job safely and quickly. And that means that you'll be able to spend more time on family, work, and fun.

For advice and assistance in assembling the following material, we turned to Bill R. Griffin, president of Cleaning Consultant Services in Seattle, which provides literature, videos, software, and seminars about cleaning.

Choose the Right Tool

When it comes to cleaning, the old shop master's rule applies: Use the right tool for the right job. The benefits are substantial.

Save time. Let's say that you need to remove adhesive tape or paint from a window. If you try to scrub it, remove it with a cleaner, or scratch it off with a knife, you're in for a long day. But with the right tool—a razor blade in a safety holder—the job will be finished in minutes.

Save money. Choosing the right cleaner sometimes means saving big bucks. For example, if you plan to scrub the mildew from your bathroom tile grout, you could buy an off-the-shelf bathroom mildew cleaner. But that can cost up to 25 cents an ounce. Making your own highly effective mildew-buster will cost just pennies. (Mix 3 tablespoons chlorine bleach with 1 quart water and put it in a spray bottle.)

Prevent damage. Follow this simple rule of thumb: Start with the gentlest cleaning methods and move on to more aggressive approaches only when the gentler means have failed. And always pretest the harsher methods in an inconspicuous spot before starting the job. Using a harsh tool or cleaning substance can damage the very thing you're trying to clean. For example, using steel wool on a stained porcelain sink could scratch the surface.

THE PH SCALE

You don't need a Ph.D. to understand the pH scale. Here's a rundown of a few products and their pH values.

pH	Product
Acidic	
0–1	Hydrochloric, sulfuric, nitric acids
1–2	Phosphoric, sulfamic acids
2.0	Citrus fruit
2.5	Carbonated drinks
3.0	Vinegar
3.7	Red wine
6.5	Milk
Neutral	
7.0	Neutral cleaners
Alkaline	
8.0	Egg whites
9.5	Soap
10.0	Baking soda
12.0	Household ammonia
12.8	Liquid household bleach
13–14	Caustic soda, floor strippers

Replacing a sink is much more expensive than using a gentler white nylon scrubbing pad from the start.

Learn the Five Basic Cleaning Chemicals

The cleaning aisle of any supermarket is packed with a stupefying array of products. But here's a little secret. There are only five basic types of cleaning chemicals. Understand them, and you'll be able to pick the right one for the job and save money in the bargain. Here's a rundown.

Surfactants. These are also listed as surface-active agents on labels. The secret behind the chemical scrubbing power of almost every cleaner on the market, surfactants create what chemists call wetting. Essentially, surfactants lower the surface tension of water on the item, making it flow more smoothly over surfaces and into tiny cracks, crevices, and pores. Once this liquid has penetrated, the other chemicals in a cleaning solution can get in there and break down soils. "Then you can wash away the soil along with the liquid," explains Mahilal Dahanayake, Ph.D., senior manager for household and industrial surfactants at Rhône-Poulenc Corporation in Princeton, New Jersey, which makes the basic surfactant chemicals that go into everything from shampoos and detergents to industrial cleaners and soaps.

Alkalies. Most cleaners contain alkalies, not acids. To understand why, you have to know a little about the pH scale. The scale, which runs from 0 to 14, is a measure of the acidity or alkalinity of a water-based solution. A value of 7 on the scale is neutral. Solutions with a value lower than 7 are acidic; those with values higher than 7 are alkaline. Substances at the far ends of the scale, such as sulfuric acid and caustic soda, are extremely aggressive and corrosive. Here's where all this is leading. Soils made of acids (and all fats and oils are made of fatty acids and glycerol) break down when combined with alkalies. And alkaline soils break down when combined with acids. Since the majority of soils—from hamburger grease to plain old mud—are acidic, most cleaners are powered with alkalies. "Alkalies actually chew up fat and oil molecules, breaking them into smaller particles that become suspended and can be washed away," Dr. Dahanayake says.

Acids. Fewer soils are alkaline, and so fewer cleaners use acidic solutions to do the dirty work. Certain soils—such as lime scale, soap deposits, rust, tannin (from coffee and tea stains), alcoholic beverages, and mustard—are alkaline and need to be attacked with an acidic cleaner. They range in strength from the mildness of a white vinegar and water solution to the harshness of sulfuric acid.

(continued on page 40)

CLEANING CHEMICALS:
WHAT'S IN THIS STUFF ANYWAY?

Here's a rundown of the common household cleaners, their ingredients, and their uses.

All-purpose cleaners

Abrasive liquids
Ingredients: Suspension of solid abrasive particles in thickened liquid, and more surfactants than in abrasive powders.
Uses: Cleansing hard surfaces like sinks, tubs, and counters susceptible to scratching by harsher abrasives.

Abrasive powders
Ingredients: Fine particles of minerals such as calcite, quartz, and silica. Also surfactants and sometimes bleach.
Uses: Removing relatively heavy amounts of soil from sturdy surfaces.

Nonabrasive powders and liquids
Ingredients: Surfactants, builders (which soften hard water and keep soil particles in suspension), and alkaline buffer salts. Sometimes disinfectants, ammonia, pine oil, and organic solvents. Usually diluted with water.
Uses: Cleaning large, washable surfaces like floors, walls, countertops, and woodwork.

Nonabrasive sprays
Ingredients: Surfactants, builders (which soften hard water and suspend particles of dirt), and organic solvents. No need to dilute.
Uses: Removing greasy soils in small areas like walls around appliances, cooktops, and switch plates.

Other Cleaning Aids

Ammonia
Ingredients: Ammonium hydroxide (Ammoniated cleaners usually are mixed with detergent.)

Uses: Since it leaves no streaks, it's good for cleaning glass and shiny appliances and removing buildup from no-wax floors. Also an effective spot remover. Do not use on clear plastic windows.

Baking soda
Ingredients: Sodium bicarbonate
Uses: Mild abrasive for cleaning softer surfaces like fiberglass. Also good for deodorizing refrigerators, freezers, and pet litter boxes.

Borax
Ingredients: Sodium borate.
Uses: Mildly alkaline water-soluble salt works as a mild abrasive. Add to laundry load to boost cleaning power.

Kitchen, Bathroom, Glass, and Metal Cleaners

Bleaches
Ingredients: Sodium hypochlorite (liquid household bleach).
Uses: Removing stains on fabrics and hard surfaces. Kills bacteria, viruses, and fungi.

Disinfectants and disinfectant cleaners
Ingredients: Antimicrobial agents such as pine oil, sodium hypochlorite, quaternary ammonium compounds, or phenols. Disinfectant cleaners contain surfactants and builders (which soften hard water and hold dirt in suspension).
Uses: Cleaning and disinfecting hard surfaces such as floors, sinks, showers, and tubs.

Drain openers
Ingredients: Some openers are formulated to reduce clog buildup. They

contain enzymes that digest organic materials. Traditional drain openers (liquid or crystal) contain powerful lyes or acids made of sodium hydroxide or sodium hypochlorite to open the blockage.
Uses: Preventing drain clogs, dissolving drain clogs.

Glass and multisurface cleaners
Ingredients: Surfactants, mild solvents, alcohol (to speed drying), and sometimes ammonia (to prevent streaking).
Uses: Cleaning glass, and cleaning and polishing chrome, stainless steel, and other brightwork.

Hard-water mineral removers
Ingredients: Spray and powder forms contain citric, oxalic, sulfamic, or hydroxyacetic acid. Also include surfactants and organic solvents.
Uses: Dissolving minerals, lime scale, and rust left behind by hard-water evaporation.

Metal cleaners and polishes
Ingredients: Mild abrasive such as kaopolite or hydrous silica and acid such as oxalic, sulfuric, or citric. Some products contain antioxidants to protect against rapid retarnishing, and surfactants.
Uses: Removing tarnish and cleaning.

Oven cleaners
Ingredients: Surfactants and a strong alkali such as sodium hydroxide (lye) or less alkaline salts (used with oven heat).
Uses: Cleaning oven interior and racks.

Toilet-bowl cleaners
Ingredients: Surfactants plus oxidants or acids; disinfecting formulas also contain antimicrobial agents such as quaternary ammonium salts.
Uses: Removing deposits, cleaning, and sometimes disinfecting.

Tub, tile, and sink cleaners
Ingredients: Surfactants and solvents. Some products contain oxidants such as sodium hypochlorite and antimicrobial agents to kill mold and mildew. Some are formulated with alkaline ingredients such as sodium carbonate, sodium silicate, and sodium hydroxide.
Uses: Removing hard-water deposits, soap scum, rust stains, and discoloration due to mold.

Floor and Furniture Products

Carpet and rug cleaners
Ingredients: Surfactant and a polymer that helps dry the product into a brittle form that can be removed by vacuuming.
Uses: Taking up oily and greasy soils from carpet.

Dusting products
Ingredients: Hydrocarbon oil that attracts dust and sometimes organic solvent and water for stain removal.
Uses: Picking up and holding dust on a cloth or applicator.

Floor-care products
Ingredients: Cleaners contain surfactants and builders (which soften hard water and keep soil particles in suspension). Products that also wax contain particles of polyethylene or carnauba and polymers, such as polyacrylate. Floor strippers contain ammonia.
Uses: Removing soil, stripping, polishing, and protecting surface.

Furniture cleaners and polishes
Ingredients: Silicone fluids, wax, lemon oil, tung oil, and hydrocarbon solvent to remove oily stains and some wax buildup.
Uses: Removing dust and stains, producing shine, protecting against water spots.

Solvents. The chemistry of solvents is different than that of alkalies or acids. Rather than neutralizing soils, solvents actually dissolve them. Almost all solvents are distilled from petroleum or plant products, and they're mostly used to dissolve oily and greasy soils and substances—everything from grass stains to oil-based varnish. Common solvents include paint thinner and lacquer thinner (derived from petroleum products), acetone, alcohol and glycerin (derived from plants and animals), and some spot removers. Though effective, solvents are often flammable, usually toxic, and also hard on the environment. For that reason, professional cleaners and the manufacturers of consumer cleaning products have been cutting back on using and selling them in the past decade.

Disinfectants. Chemical disinfectants have the ability to kill germs. For the most part, this involves wiping out the germs that cause odors, stain clothes, spoil food, and cause disease. (Some germs, like the bacteria in your stomach, are necessary for health.) Products that are sold as disinfectants must be registered with the Environmental Protection Agency before they can be sold. There are three main disinfectants you can buy for home use. The most common kind of cleaning disinfectants are called quaternary ammonium compounds. Quats, as the professionals call them, can be combined easily with detergents that pack a pH of 9 to 10 without losing their germ-killing power. That's why you'll find them in bathroom and kitchen cleaners like Lysol Antibacterial Kitchen Cleaner.

Don't try to make your own disinfectants at home. Combining chemicals can be tricky. You run the risk of destroying the germ-killing effects of the chemicals. And there's also the very real danger of creating toxic or volatile mixtures. Other common disinfectants include liquid household bleach (like Clorox), and some pine oil cleaners with natural pine oil also qualify as disinfectants.

To Master Messes, Get Mobile

It's very easy to put together a cleaning kit that's portable and has the right stuff for swabbing up about 90 percent of household messes. Think of it as the light infantry in your cleaning army, says John Becker, sales manager at Easterday Janitorial Supply Company in San Francisco, one of the West Coast's largest janitorial companies.

Your cleaning kit should be neatly packed in an organized box or, better yet, a plastic cleaning caddy, which can be easily picked up and whisked off to the scene of the grime. Becker, who teaches janitors about the tools of their trade, advises them to stock a cleaning kit with three basic strategies in mind. The advice works just as well at home.

Protect yourself. Scrubbing and using cleaning chemicals can be hard on your hands and potentially dangerous for your eyes. So your cleaning kit should include a sturdy pair of rubber gloves and a pair of safety glasses that you can use when necessary.

Stock the basic cleaners. Becker and other experts recommend stocking your kit with just three cleaning products: an all-purpose cleaner (a mild one such as liquid dishwashing detergent or Fantastik), a glass cleaner (like Windex), and a disinfectant cleaner (like Lysol Antibacterial Kitchen Cleaner). To make the kit complete for taking on a bathroom, add a spray bottle with a freshly prepared solution of 1 quart water and 3 tablespoons chlorine bleach, and a good toilet-bowl cleaner (which contains a fairly acidic cleaner and should only be used in the toilet bowl). Do not mix cleaning products.

Carry scrubbers. Your kit should include a sponge with a nylon scrubber backing that's white or tan, which indicates mild abrasiveness that's safe for most surfaces. Throw in a good nylon scrub brush and your basic cleaning kit is complete.

Smart Solutions

Now it's time to take your cleaning campaign to a new level. Here are some tool-savvy strategies that will help you save time, money, and effort while cleaning around the house.

Find Quick Fixes at Your Fingertips

For generations, common household items—from vinegar and baking soda to cola and rubbing alcohol—have been used in a pinch as cleaners and spot removers. In many cases, they work well. In some cases, you're better off reaching for a good basic cleaner like liquid dishwashing detergent. Here's the real story, and some cautions, on how to use some common household items.

Alcohol. Isopropyl alcohol is a solvent that will remove many types of dye stains from fabric. Be careful, though. It can also make the dye you want to stay in the fabric run. Test it in an inconspicuous place first, especially with silk and acetate.

Cola. In a pinch, the phosphoric acid in cola will clean alkaline soils like those found inside a toilet bowl. But beware: The sugar and caramel coloring can leave stains if left to dry on a surface.

Hair spray. Because it contains alcohol and other solvents and resins, hair spray will dissolve ink. You may wish to use men's unscented hair spray to get stains off vinyl. Cheaper brands of hair spray actually work the best. It is useful as a laundry pretreater for ink stains. But make sure that you launder any fabric after using hair spray since it can stiffen the fabric permanently.

Meat tenderizer. The enzymes "digest" stains from foods such as meat, eggs, blood, and milk, which are made up mainly of protein. Enzymes sold as cleaners work as well or better, and they don't contain the spices and coloring of a meat tenderizer.

Nail polish remover. Nail polish remover contains the solvent amyl acetate and sometimes acetone. Just as it will remove polish from your fingernails, it can also remove it from fabrics. It can also remove model airplane glue. But be cautious: Some nail polish removers contain oil that can leave a stain of its own on fabric. And the solvents will destroy acetate fabrics.

Reach Out for Those Distant Nooks and Crannies

The nice thing about hard-to-reach places is that it's harder for dirt and grime to reach them, too. Still, the dust and dirt circulating indoors will find their way to ceilings, high windows, beams, molding, cracks, and crevices. There are two basic approaches to getting the out-of-the-way soils where they live.

Reach it. Start the attack with a tool that can do the reaching for you. One of the best is the extension wand on your vacuum cleaner. Use the brush attachment to loosen cobwebs and dust and to reach behind furniture and appliances. You can buy extra lengths of extension pipe at a good vacuum repair shop.

Another great reaching tool is the telescoping extension handle available in most hardware stores and janitorial supply stores. This pole extends up to 12 feet and is designed to hold squeegees and brushes.

Climb to it. There are three solid approaches here, with the emphasis on solid. For stretching only slightly beyond your normal reach, use a very sturdy step stool or sturdy, reinforced wooden box. For climbing the higher heights, use a lightweight stepladder. The best choice is a 5-foot aluminum model. It's sturdy, lightweight, and high enough to reach 8-foot ceilings but not so tall as to crash into doorways and walls when you're carrying it from room to room. For jobs that require extended time on high, assemble a temporary scaffolding by supporting a sturdy, 2-inch-thick plank on the level between the box and the stepladder (or between two stepladders). This allows you to clean the length of an entire room without having to climb up and down a ladder.

Clean Those Cleaning Tools, Too

Of course, cleaning tools need cleaning and maintenance themselves. After all, they get down and dirty with the grime. For some tools, the cleanup should be done at the time of use. For example, rinse out buckets, mops, and sponges when you're through cleaning. Launder cleaning cloths and even your favorite cleaning outfits separately; the extra grime they carry should be kept away from your everyday wash. And speaking of laundry, keep your dryer's lint filter clean so that the air inside flows efficiently.

Other tools need regular maintenance. Consider, for example, the vacuum cleaner. The bag must be changed regularly, and you should periodically clean thread and hair from the beater brush (the cylindrical brush that rolls against the carpet) and make sure that it's in good shape.

Tools and Materials from A to Z

Here's an A-to-Z rundown of everything you will need to know about how to buy and use household cleaning materials and tools. Note the cautions we've provided, too. Some of these cleaning materials can damage your possessions or be toxic to you.

Abrasive Cleaners

Uses: Abrasive cleaners contain small particles of grit that help dislodge soil from a surface. These particles do the grinding. Most abrasive cleaners—from scouring powder to toothpaste—also contain chemicals that help the cleaning along. Color-coded nylon scrub pads, like Scotch-Brite, are filled with abrasives. Brown and black are the scratchiest; blue and green are slightly less abrasive; red is medium; and white, tan, and yellow pads are the least abrasive. Use the white pads only to avoid scratching surfaces, advises Bill R. Griffin, president of Cleaning Consultant Services in Seattle, which provides literature, videos, software, and seminars about cleaning.

Use abrasives on tougher materials that resist scratching. Sinks, tile showers, tubs, and toilets can be cleaned safely with most modern-formulation liquid scouring cleansers. Still, abrasives can cause microscratches and dull finishes. It's best to turn to abrasives only after gentler methods fail, and always use the gentlest abrasive first. It's also smart to test abrasives on an inconspicuous spot before tackling the whole job.

Maybe it's the get-tough approach that makes abrasive cleaners a favorite of the military. Powdered cleansers are one of the three basic cleaning tools used in the U.S. Marines, says retired Gunnery Sergeant Sylvia Gethicker, formerly stationed at Camp LeJeune in North Carolina (the other Marine standbys are glass cleaner and all-purpose cleaner). Thoroughly rinsing sinks and toilets is an important part of using abrasive powders properly, Sergeant

HOW DOES YOUR CLEANING ARSENAL STACK UP?

Here's a checklist of the cleaning items every house should have, says Bill R. Griffin, president of Cleaning Consultant Services in Seattle, which provides literature, videos, software, and seminars about cleaning.

▸ Abrasive-backed sponge (white)

▸ All-purpose cleaner

▸ Bowl caddy and toilet brush

▸ Carpet spotter (without optical brighteners)

▸ Disinfectant cleaner

▸ Glass and surface cleaner

▸ Kitchen broom

▸ Lamb's wool duster

▸ Neutral cleaner

▸ Rubber gloves

▸ Sponge mop

▸ Spray bottles

▸ Squeegee

▸ Terry towels (white)

▸ Upright vacuum

Gethicker says. "If I rub my hand over it and there's a powder residue, that wouldn't be considered clean," she says. "The trick is that you don't use too much and that you rinse well."

How to buy: For tougher jobs, buy liquid cleansers that contain bleach. The differences between brands are minimal, so look for the best price. The liquids also have the advantage of squirting easily into harder-to-reach spots like the rim of a toilet bowl.

Caution: By their very nature, abrasives can scratch and dull even hard surfaces like porcelain or enamel. They will damage mirror-finish stainless steel, fiberglass, laminated surfaces such as Formica, and cultured marble countertops. Use gentler methods first. Also, as with any cleaner that contains bleach, it's important not to mix bleach cleansers with ammonia products because toxic fumes will result.

Absorbents

Uses: Usually made of powdery or granular materials, absorbents work like slow-acting natural vacuum cleaners. When placed on a stain or porous material, they absorb the spill so that you can sweep, vacuum, or brush it away.

Use absorbents on fresh stains—especially grease and oil—that are still damp. In many cases, you should blot them and place a dry washcloth or towel over the stain. Then place a book or some other household item on it to hold the towel in place, and leave the absorbents to do their sponge-like work for several hours and as long as overnight.

Absorbents are often a good first step for eliminating a stain before you resort to stronger methods. They can work on the nastiest messy spills, like engine oil on a driveway or vomit on a carpet. Cat litter or sawdust is a good absorbent for these jobs. For more delicate situations, like pulling up a gravy stain from a dry-clean-only wool blazer, absorbents such as talcum powder or cornstarch can be effective. Salt works for lifting flavored drink mix such as Kool-Aid (and stains from ice pops or fruit-flavored gelatins) from carpet and clothes.

How to buy: Commercial preparations are available, but in many cases the household items like talcum powder, cornmeal, and salt work just as well. For bigger, messy cleanups, buy regular cat litter (not the clumping kind) or a commercial product like Quicksorb.

Caution: If you use an absorbent outside, be sure to remove it before it gets tracked inside or blown into flower beds (or your neighbor's yard). Be careful using talcum powder and cornstarch on fabric. They're sometimes hard to remove.

Acidic Cleaners

Most cleaners use mildly alkaline chemicals to do the dirty work. That's because most soils are acidic, which is on the other end of the pH scale. Alkalies neutralize acids, and the rest is cleaning history. But a few stains and soils are alkaline, and for those you need cleaners with acid to do the neutralizing. Acid cleaners range from substances as benign as white vinegar to compounds as corrosive and dangerous as sulfuric acid. Always read product labels for proper use and safety precautions. Here's a rundown of the seven most common types of acid cleaners.

Acetic (Vinegar)

Uses: Undiluted, it works to remove mild amounts of lime in coffeepots and teapots, it rinses, and it neutralizes the residue of alkaline cleaners.

How to buy: Clear white distilled vinegar is best. Wine and cider vinegars can leave stains.

Caution: Vinegar can weaken the fibers in cotton, linen, and acetate.

Citric (Lemon Juice)

Uses: As a stain remover, it functions as a mild bleach. It also can remove stains from coffeepots and teapots, but it takes longer.

How to buy: Simply pick up some fresh lemons at the grocery store and squeeze their juice. (By the way, lemons squeezed at room temperature produce about twice as much juice as refrigerated lemons.) You can also buy it in bottled form at the grocery store.

Caution: Lemon juice may tarnish metals.

Oxalic

Uses: A gentler acid for removing rust stains, it has a bleaching effect.

How to buy: See the ingredients on the product label. You can find it at janitorial supply stores.

Caution: It is poisonous if ingested. Always read product labels for proper use and safety precautions.

Phosphoric

Uses: It's a component in toilet-bowl cleaners, tub-and-tile cleaners, lime descalers, metal polishes, and denture cleaners. It's also an ingredient in most soft drinks.

How to buy: Check the ingredients list on the product label. You can also purchase it at janitorial supply stores.

Caution: Phosphoric acid can damage surfaces if not rinsed immediately after use. It's also a mild skin and mucous membrane irritant. It is best to avoid breathing its fumes. Wear rubber gloves.

Hydrochloric

Uses: An ingredient in some toilet-bowl and drain cleaners, it's also used to clean mineral deposits from quarry tile floors and to etch concrete floors before sealing.

How to buy: Check the ingredients list on the product label. You can also purchase it at janitorial supply stores.

Caution: Hydrochloric acid is very corrosive and, at greater concentrations, poisonous. It will damage skin and mucous membranes. Avoid breathing fumes, and wear rubber gloves when using. It also bleaches nylon and dissolves cotton and rayon, so be especially careful using it around carpet. It can also weaken the binders in cement. This is nasty stuff. Avoid using it if you can.

Sulfuric

Uses: An ingredient in some toilet-bowl and drain cleaners, this powerful acid attacks and corrodes most organic substances, nylon, and vinyl.

How to buy: You can purchase it at janitorial supply stores.

Caution: Sulfuric acid is extremely corrosive. It damages eyes and mucous membranes on contact and eats skin in seconds. The fumes released when the acid reacts with organic matter (in drainpipes) can contain noxious gases, so be sure that the room is well-ventilated. The heat produced in drainpipes is sometimes enough to crack or melt pipes. This is nasty stuff. Avoid using it if you can.

Hydrofluoric

Uses: It is used in rust and lime-scale removers and commercial rust removers.

How to buy: You can find it at janitorial supply stores.

CLEAN UP WITH NEUTRAL CONCENTRATES

It may not be fancy, but concentrated neutral cleaner is perfect for most daily cleaning needs—everything from floor mopping to wall washing. This is a cleaning product that has a neutral pH, or a pH around 7. It's safe for most surfaces and fabrics and doesn't leave streaks. And by getting it in its undiluted form, you can save money and save room in your storage closet. Buy it at a janitorial supply store and dilute according to the directions.

Caution: Hydrofluoric acid etches porcelain and glass. It quickly burns skin, so use rubber gloves, goggles, and extra caution. Always read product labels for proper use and safety precautions. This is nasty stuff. Avoid using it if you can.

Alcohol

Uses: A fairly pure solvent, alcohol is an effective antiseptic (it's what gives hospital waiting rooms their peculiar odor) and also a good cleaner.

Alcohol cuts grease and works well for cleaning the smudges and fingerprints from windows (mix one part alcohol with four parts water and apply with a cloth and rinse clean with a squeegee). It's a common ingredient in many glass cleaners because it dries quickly and leaves no streaks. Alcohol also dissolves body oils and makeup on shiny jewelry (although it will dissolve and damage lacquered metal jewelry). Alcohol works well as a stain remover. It will get rid of grass stains, pencil, some inks, and some dyes. As with all spot removers, be sure to pretest an inconspicuous area of fabric or surface to make sure that the cleaner causes no damage. In a pinch, alcohol will also help dissolve and remove the adhesive of stickers on windows or hard surfaces.

How to buy: Look for denatured or isopropyl alcohol at drugstores. Avoid rubbing alcohol, which can contain dyes, perfumes, and excessive water.

Caution: Isopropyl alcohol is poisonous and flammable. It should be used only in a well-ventilated area and never around open flames (including pilot lights). As a solvent, it can dissolve plastics and adhesives. It can also damage certain fabrics. Don't use it on wool. For silk and acetates, dilute it by half with water. Always read product labels for proper use and safety precautions.

Alkali Cleaners

Because most common messes are acidic (they have a value of less than 7 on the pH scale), the vast majority of cleaners are alkaline. Remember that alkalies neutralize acids. Once neutralized, the soil (be it hamburger grease or a kid's handprint) can be rinsed away more easily.

The variety of alkaline cleaners is mind-numbing. Everything from liquid dishwashing detergent and glass cleaner to caustic lye drain openers and wax strippers can be classified as alkaline cleaners. Manufacturers use various alkaline chemicals as the basis for most of their products. These chemicals include sodium hydroxide and sodium metasilicate (strong alkalies), sodium carbonate (baking soda), and the old standby ammonia, which works especially well as a floor cleaner because it is very effective at removing wax finish. Here's an overview of the spectrum of alkali cleaning products.

pH: 12–14

Uses: The strongest alkalies are effective for heavy-duty cleaning and stain removal.

Products: These chemicals are used in oven cleaners, lye drain openers, automatic dishwasher detergents, wax strippers, degreasers, and heavy-duty cleaners.

Caution: Be extremely careful when using these heavy-duty cleaners. Their strong alkalinity can damage skin and mucous membranes, so be sure to wear rubber gloves and safety glasses. They can also damage paint, aluminum, copper, and silk and wool fabrics. Fumes can be caustic, so make sure that the area you are working in is well-ventilated. Wear gloves and safety glasses.

pH: 9–12

Uses: These milder products are excellent for general cleaning and won't damage surfaces and fabrics the way stronger cleaners can.

Products: Laundry detergent, all-purpose cleaners, and glass and multisurface cleaners are among the cleaners that contain middle-range alkalies.

Caution: These products can damage delicate fabrics. At the same time, they may not have the cleaning ferocity needed for tougher jobs.

pH: 7–9

Uses: The neutral-to-mildest alkalies are safe for almost all surfaces and fabrics. They're especially good for light-duty jobs like floor mopping and wall washing.

Products: Liquid dishwashing detergents, neutral cleaners, and mild laundry detergents such as Woolite contain these mild chemicals.

Caution: These products may not have the cleaning ferocity needed for tougher jobs.

All-Purpose Cleaners

All-purpose cleaners are the foot soldiers of any household general's cleaning army. They are the first line of offense you should try before resorting to the heavy artillery. Why? An all-purpose cleaner's mildness won't damage most surfaces and fabrics. They come in several formulations and have various attributes—from the relative strength of spray cleaners like Formula 409 or Fantastik to the mildness of a fine fabric detergent like Woolite. Most are mildly to moderately alkaline (because they're cleaning up acidic soils like grease and dirt). And most lack the special attributes required to clean windows and ovens or to remove mildew. Their virtue lies in their versatility. Here's a walk down the all-purpose aisle.

Concentrates

Uses: The basics: washing floors, counters, walls—anywhere that gets some dirt but not built-up grime. Concentrates are cleaners that need to be diluted with water before you use them. Cleaners in this form are cheaper, require less packaging, and are lighter in your grocery bag. One of the safest all-purpose cleaners is plain old liquid dishwashing detergent. Another mild all-purpose liquid, neutral cleaner, is available in concentrated form at any janitorial supply store. Many contain pine oil, which in higher concentrations can work as a disinfectant. (Look for the Environmental Protection Agency registration notice on the label, designating it as a disinfectant.) It also smells nice and clean. Products with higher concentrations of ammonia may fall into this category, but they're generally high enough in alkalinity to be considered heavy-duty cleaners.

How to buy: The choices are vast. So stick with a relatively inexpensive brand that works for you. Most of the cleaners contain the same basic ingredients: surfactants, builders and alkaline buffer, and sometimes, disinfectant pine oil.

Caution: Don't rely on all-purpose cleaners for effective germ killing. Most don't contain enough disinfectant chemical to do much more than wipe out a few million of the malicious microbes—and that's just scratching the surface.

Spray Cleaners

Uses: Aim these handy cleaners, like Formula 409, at smaller washable areas like soiled switch plates, chrome fixtures, appliances, and nonglass cooktops. (You can get special cleaners for glass cooktops from kitchen appliance stores.) Spray on, then quickly wipe off. Some of the most popular sprays contain alkaline chemicals that push them into the heavy-duty cleaner

A STROKE OF GENIUS

When you've swept as much hay, sawdust, and horse dung as Pete Cimini and his crew have, you learn a few tricks for making the job easier. One of the best, says Cimini, stable manager for the Ringling Bros. and Barnum and Bailey Circus, headquartered in Vienna, Virginia, is the technique he uses to sweep large areas.

It's simple. Don't start at one side of the large area, sweep a long row, and then trudge back to sweep another long row. Instead:

1. Start in one corner, sweep one long stroke, about the length of your arm.

2. Step sideways to make another long stroke. Continue moving sideways after each stroke.

3. When you reach the other side of the area you're sweeping, step forward one broom stroke and work your way back toward the other side.

"Try it," Cimini says. "You'll save a lot of time by not walking back and forth."

range. When using a spray cleaner on a surface for the first time—especially painted surfaces—test on an inconspicuous spot first.

How to buy: Mix your own in a quart spray bottle using concentrated cleaner that you can buy in a janitorial supply store, or find a brand off the shelf that works for you.

Caution: Stronger spray cleaners can take the finish off furniture and soften or discolor paint, especially when left on more than a minute or so. When mixing your own spray from concentrate, make sure that you measure the proportions correctly. A too-strong preparation will be harsher and won't rinse as easily.

Ammonia

Uses: Ammonia is one of those basic cleaning chemicals that shows up in lots of products and does many different jobs. Here's a look at three of ammonia's biggest duties in the cleaning world.

General Cleaning

Ammonia cleaners usually come formulated with a detergent to make them sudsy and help mask the strong vapors that ammonia (ammonium hydroxide) gives off. Ammonia helps boost a cleaner's alkalinity, which makes it a decent grease-cutter.

Use ammoniated cleaners for no-wax floors, walls, and light-duty bathroom cleaning. The usual mixture is about ½ cup ammonia per gallon of water. Stronger mixtures of ammonia are also effective for stripping wax floors. For bigger degreasing jobs (like range hoods), use a product such as Formula 409. One other hint: Those smelly ammonia fumes can be put to good use. A pan of ammonia left in the oven overnight will make oven cleaning easier. Remember not to turn the oven on and to be careful when opening the oven door because of ammonia's strong fumes.

Window Cleaning

Because ammonia is what chemists call a volatile alkali, it leaves no solid residue as it dries. That's why it's a staple in glass-cleaning products and some specialty cleaners for shiny surfaces. It puts the "free" in "streak-free." You can make your own glass cleaner using a solution of 1 ounce clear ammonia to 1 quart water. Dispense it with a pump sprayer or apply and remove it with a sponge or squeegee.

Spot Removal

Ammonia has a mild bleaching action, which makes it an effective spot remover for many soils, surfaces, and fabrics. To make a spotting solution, combine 1 tablespoon household ammonia with ½ cup water. It will help remove spots caused by a wide range of items, including alcoholic beverages, ink, mustard, and tomato sauce.

How to buy: Versatile clear ammonia is available at janitorial supply stores and grocery stores. At the grocery store and drugstore, read ingredient labels to find cleaning and glass products that contain ammonia.

Caution: Use caution when using ammonia. It is poisonous if swallowed, and the fumes can harm mucous membranes in your nasal passages, eyes, throat, and lungs. So make sure that the area you are cleaning is well-ventilated. Be sure to use rubber gloves and safety glasses when cleaning with ammonia because it can irritate the skin. Never mix ammonia with household bleach products—the combination can cause toxic fumes.

Ammonia takes the wax finish off floors, so don't use it on a waxed floor unless you want to strip it. Dilute it according to directions and wear rubber gloves. Use in a well-ventilated area. Ammonia can also harm varnished surfaces, marble, soft plastic, and leather. Ammonia will darken aluminum pans, so don't soak them in it. It can also alter the color of some dyes, so before using it as a spot remover, test on an inconspicuous spot. Ammonia will cause browning of some upholstery fabrics and natural-fiber carpets and rugs. Always read product labels for proper use and safety precautions.

Baking Soda

Uses: It's named for its ability to make baked goods rise, but that's just the beginning of baking soda's usefulness. Sodium bicarbonate (baking soda's chemical name) turns out to be an adequate replacement for many household cleaners. And it's finding new converts today, says John Becker, sales manager at Easterday Janitorial Supply Company in San Francisco, one of the West Coast's largest janitorial companies. "We're going back to the way Grandma used to clean," he says. "She wasn't too bad off using household cleaners like baking soda."

Baking soda is mildly alkaline, gently abrasive, and safe on most surfaces and fabrics. There are three basic cleaning uses for baking soda: It boosts cleaning and bleaching in laundering, works as a gently abrasive cleaner and stain remover on hard surfaces, and can be used as a deodorizer in lots of places.

Baking soda does clean, but it doesn't have the cleaning oomph of a detergent. So experiment with different surfaces and soils to figure out whether baking soda is up to the job. Although baking soda brings out the shine in most metals, it won't shine aluminum surfaces.

Laundry booster: To improve cleaning and help deodorize, add ½ cup baking soda to liquid laundry detergent to help whiten socks and other light durable fabrics. You can also reduce the use of chlorine bleach by using baking soda. Instead of using a full cup of bleach, use ½ cup regular bleach and ½ cup baking soda to boost bleaching action.

Hard-surface cleaning: For light cleaning of kitchen and bathroom surfaces, make a solution of 4 tablespoons baking soda to 1 quart warm water and wipe, using a cleaning cloth. Then rinse. For tougher hard-surface jobs, mix up a paste using equal parts baking soda and warm water. You can also mix up a poultice of baking soda and water that, when left on for an hour or so, will pull stains from china, porcelain, countertops, and other hard surfaces.

Deodorizing: Baking soda absorbs odors in the refrigerator, in carpet, and in pet areas. To deodorize a refrigerator, take the top completely off a box and leave it inside at the back of a shelf. You can also leave an open box in musty closets or storage areas. Change them every 3 months. For carpets, sprinkle directly on, allow it to sit about 15 minutes, and vacuum. To keep litter box odor to a minimum, sprinkle baking soda in the box before adding the litter.

How to buy: Even name-brand baking soda is quite inexpensive, but store brands and generics are generally cheaper and equally pure, says Becker. Just make sure that the label says USP, which means that it meets United States Pharmacopeia purity standards.

Bleach

Uses: When people speak of bleach, they usually mean chlorine bleach like liquid Clorox bleach. But there are other bleaches, including hydrogen peroxide (the same stuff you put on cuts and scrapes) and oxygen bleach (nonchlorine "all-fabric" bleaches such as Clorox 2). Ammonia, lemon juice, and white vinegar also can remove specific stains. Why does chlorine bleach seem to get all the attention? It's the most effective and powerful by far.

Used according to label directions, chlorine bleach is a great whitener and brightener for laundry. It's also the bleach that disinfects. Use it only on whites and colorfast fabrics. (If you're not sure about colorfastness, pretest using a solution of 1 tablespoon bleach in ¼ cup water. Using a cotton swab, dab a drop on an inside seam. Wait 1 minute, then blot dry with a paper towel. If no color comes off on the towel, the fabric can be washed safely in liquid bleach.) Be sure to test all colors and decorative trim.

Chlorine bleach removes the color from stains in fabrics and whitens. In addition to gentle beaching action, all-fabric bleaches often have enzymes (to remove stains) and brighteners (to keep clothes looking new). You can also use chlorine bleach to pretreat stubborn stains such as tough baby and toddler stains, says Sandy Sullivan, manager of marketing and environmental communications, and spokesperson for the Clorox Company in Oakland, California.

Check for colorfastness and check the label to see if the fabric can be bleached. Soak the whole garment for about 5 minutes in a solution of ¼ cup bleach and 1 gallon cool water. If it's a two-piece outfit, soak both pieces.

Chlorine bleach works especially well to kill and remove mildew in the bathroom. Dilute it (¾ cup per gallon of water), put it in a spray bottle, and go to work spritzing the tile. Let it sit for 3 to 5 minutes, then scrub with a white scrubbing pad. Be sure to rinse all surfaces thoroughly, and ventilate the room well during cleaning. Bleach breaks down quickly, so mix a fresh batch each time and discard any leftover solution.

How to buy: As a cleaning agent, there's little difference between brands of bleaches, so look for the best buy. But if disinfection is important to you, look for the word "disinfectant" on the label, which means that it's registered with the Environmental Protection Agency.

Caution: Never mix chlorine bleach with other household cleaners, especially ammonia. Toxic fumes can result. Read and carefully follow the product label for proper use and safety precautions.

Use chlorine bleach to brighten laundry or remove stains. Never use chlorine bleach on wool, silk, mohair, leather, Spandex, noncolorfast fabrics, or rugs or carpets. Don't use undiluted bleach; always follow the label instructions.

Borax

Uses: Borax is a mildly alkaline, water-soluble salt. This white crystalline stuff appears as an ingredient in some detergents and heavy-duty hand-washing formulations. Borax can be mixed with water and used as a household cleaner. Most often, though, it's added to laundry to boost cleaning power. When you're laundering diapers, borax can help eliminate odors. You can also add a teaspoon or so to automatic dishwasher detergent to increase alkalinity and improve cleaning.

How to buy: The white crystals are incorporated in small amounts in some laundry detergents and many diaper presoak products. Look for it on the label. You can also find pure borax as a laundry additive at grocery stores and drugstores.

Caution: As a household cleaner, borax isn't as effective as detergent or all-purpose cleaner. Some hand-washing formulations can be hard on your skin. Follow the product label for proper use and safety precautions.

Brooms

Uses: Sure, it's incredibly primitive in design, but there's still nothing handier than a broom for efficiently removing debris from smooth floors, patios, and driveways. Brooms are also good for sweeping out carpeted corners and edges before vacuuming.

For relatively small floors, and to prepare carpet for vacuuming, use an angled nylon broom. It can reach into corners better, the split-tip bristles pick up even fine dirt, and the angled end allows more of the broom to come comfortably into contact with the floor.

For outdoor sweeping and for rough surfaces, use a push broom with hard bristles of plastic, nylon, or bassine fiber.

How to buy: For indoor brooms, avoid the type with traditional straw-like bristles—they tend to shed bristles. Instead, look for an angled broom with nylon bristles. They're relatively inexpensive, especially at warehouse home supply stores, so buy several to keep in different parts of your home. Hang a broom by the ring or the hole at the end of the handle so that it doesn't stand on its bristles. For push jobs that require finer bristles, choose a broom with harder plastic bristles around the perimeter of the broom head and softer nylon in the center.

Caution: When using a push broom, remember to switch the handle from your left to your right side every few minutes to avoid strain and fatigue on one side. When practical, use a vacuum instead of a broom. It's better for indoor air quality and does a more thorough job of cleaning.

Brushes—Scrub, Wire

Uses: For cleaning an object or surface with a pitted, variable, or meshed surface, a sturdy brush is the tool of choice. The idea is to reach between the cracks and crevices. Use a scrub brush with synthetic bristles to get into the grout between tiles and into the crevices in a range or stove top. On the other hand, wire brushes should be reserved for sturdy hard surfaces, like barbecue grills. They can also be used as a first pass at paint removal.

How to buy: Home supply stores carry scrub and wire brushes. Look for scrub brushes with synthetic or natural bristles, one-piece plastic backings, and comfortable handles. Buy wire brushes with sturdy wooden or plastic handles.

Caution: Make sure that you match the brush to the surface to be cleaned. A too-stiff brush can damage delicate surfaces. A too-soft brush may be damaged by a rough surface. Don't forget to thoroughly rinse scrub brushes after use, before the grime dries on the bristles and makes it harder to use next time.

Buckets

Uses: One of the basic cleaning tools, buckets should be used to hold cleaning and rinsing solutions—separately. A bucket is invaluable for mopping and can also be used to hold a cleaning solution for general household cleaning.

How to buy: Plastic buckets with sturdy handles are best. Metal buckets can dent and corrode. Also, square buckets are more stable and can also more easily accommodate a self-wringing mop.

Caution: Be sure to rinse and dry a bucket after use. Moisture and soil left inside provide a perfect environment for mold and bacteria growth.

Caddies

Uses: A caddy is like a cleaning ambulance: It rushes needed equipment to the scene of the accident. Keep the basic cleaning tools in your caddy (see "To Master Messes, Get Mobile" on page 40), and store it in a place that you can get to easily.

How to buy: Hardware and janitorial supply stores carry caddies. Because they're inexpensive (generally under $10), it's worth having more than one so that your cleaning supplies are never far from the action.

Stock an inexpensive caddy with the basic cleaning tools, and store it in a accessible place.

Chamois

Uses: These absorbent tanned sheepskins are the perfect tool for lint-free drying of everything from cars to windows. You must dampen a chamois before it can be used.

How to buy: Hardware stores and auto supply stores usually have a good selection.

Caution: Make sure that you wash it in warm, mild soapy water after use. Detergents will remove the essential oil. Just gently squeeze until damp, then dry on a flat surface.

Cloths

Uses: For general light-duty cleaning, nothing beats a soft cloth. Use it for dusting, wiping, and the final shine-up. To get more cleaning surface out of a cloth, fold a hand towel-size cloth several times so that it fits comfortably in your hand. When the surface gets dirty, turn it over. Continue unfolding until all surfaces are dirty, then switch to a new cloth.

How to buy: The key is cotton because it's absorbent. Synthetic fabrics like nylon, polyester, and rayon are engineered not to absorb. Diapers, flannel, and old T-shirts work well. You can also buy squares of cotton at most hardware stores. White terry towels are best since they are very absorbent and there's no danger that the fabric's dye will come off on what you're cleaning.

Caution: Remember to wash your cleaning cloths after use or they'll become dense and gritty with soil and cleaning chemicals. Just throw them in the washing machine with some bleach.

Club Soda

Uses: Since club soda contains a little bit of citric acid, you can use it in a pinch as a spot remover for alkaline spills such as coffee, tea, and alcohol. White vinegar and water is cheaper and more effective.

How to buy: You know—the beverages aisle at the supermarket.

Caution: Make sure that the fizzy drink you use is plain club soda. Many clear, carbonated waters around today contain sugary flavorings that can stain and soil fabric.

Cola

Uses: For emergency jobs, the phosphoric acid in drinks like Coke and Pepsi will work as a fairly effective cleaner on things with alkaline soils, such as toilet bowls and whitewall tires.

How to buy: Generic cola is cheapest and has just as much acid as the name brands.

Caution: The caramel coloring and sugar can cause stains of their own. Regular phosphoric acid cleaners are better.

Concentrates

Uses: Just like their diluted cousins, concentrates work for glass cleaning, heavy-duty cleaning, disinfectant cleaning, and where a neutral cleaner is best (light-duty cleaning with minimal residue). Mix the concentrate with water in a spray bottle.

How to buy: Ounce for ounce, concentrated cleaners are much cheaper than the diluted ones you'll find on grocery store shelves. Most janitorial supply stores will sell concentrates to the general public. Find one that will extend its wholesale price to you.

Caution: Make sure that you measure the right amount of concentrate. Excess chemical will leave residue. Also, pour water in the spray bottle first, then add the chemical. This minimizes oversudsing and protects against chemical splashes. Read the product label carefully for proper usage and safety precautions.

Copper Cleaners

Uses: Like brass, bronze, and silver, copper tarnishes. Copper cleaners and polishes remove the tarnish and renew the shine.

How to buy: There are two types: polish and cleaner. Polish usually comes in a cream or paste form. It's better at restoring a high gloss. For cookware and items with lots of details and grooves, choose a rinse-off type cleaner. Both are available at hardware stores, most grocery stores, and at janitorial supply stores.

Caution: It's especially important to remove any green tarnish (called verdigris) from the interior of copper cookware. It's toxic. Wear rubber gloves.

Detergents

Uses: Detergents were developed to do the same job as soap—dispersing and suspending dirty stuff—without forming insoluble "soap curd." You'll use very different detergents to do three different kinds of cleaning: dishwashing by hand, dishwashing by machine, and laundering.

Automatic dishwasher detergent: This detergent is a strong, even harsh cleaner that's usually quite alkaline (12–14 on the pH scale). It does an excellent job of helping to sanitize dishes in the dishwasher. It can also be used for a few heavy-duty cleaning jobs, like soaking electronic air filter collector cells from heating and cooling units.

Liquid dishwashing detergent: This is the mildest kind of detergent. It's an almost-neutral cleaner (the pH is slightly on the alkaline side of neutral) and is designed to cut grease and lift soil, then rinse easily. It also makes an ideal light-duty cleaner for any washable surface.

Laundry detergent: Laundry detergent comes in a bewildering array of formulations—with bleach, with enzymes, phosphate, nonphosphate, liquid, and powder. As you might guess, the differences among them are minimal. "They're tinkering at the margins," says Mahilal Dahanayake, Ph.D., senior manager for household and industrial surfactants at Rhône-Poulenc Corporation in Princeton, New Jersey. "Advertising plays a big part." That said, powdered detergents are more effective than liquids in preventing minerals such as iron from staining laundry.

How to buy: A little trial and error is the best way to find a brand that works for you. Put a premium on low price.

Caution: When using liquid dishwashing detergent for general cleaning, don't use too much; it will create excessive suds. When using automatic dishwasher detergent for heavy-duty cleaning, use gloves to protect your hands.

Dishwashers

Uses: Not only are dishwashers convenient but also they sanitize dishes more thoroughly than it is possible to do with human hands. Today's models can handle most of the rinsing, washing, and drying that would otherwise have to be done by hand. They often use less hot water than hand washing, too. Some even come with built-in disposals that chop and grind rinsed-off food particles.

You can also use dishwashers to wash items that you can't put in the washing machine, such as baseball-type caps. Just put the cap in a plastic hat holder (available at home, hardware, and even some grocery stores) and place it in the upper rack. Wash separately on a short wash cycle using cool or warm water.

How to buy: Most major manufacturer's dishwashers work fairly well doing the basic cleaning. Look for a model with heavier-gauge coated wire racks and a quality sound-dampening package. Extra spraying arms ensure more thorough washing. For most families, the economy model with the basic "normal," "light wash," and "rinse only" cycles will do nicely. A booster heater is a handy feature; it will automatically heat incoming water if hot water is in short supply.

Caution: Be careful about subjecting fine crystal or china, especially that with gold trim, to the rigors of the automatic dishwasher. The harsh detergents can remove the trim and etch and damage these dishes. To avoid etching everyday glassware, be sure not to use excessive detergent, especially if you have soft water. As a rule, use 1 teaspoon detergent per 20 milligrams (of minerals—usually calcium and magnesium) per liter of water hardness. Your water company can tell the hardness rating for your water. Soft water is 0 to 60 milligrams per liter, moderately hard is 61 to 120 milligrams, hard is 121 to 180 milligrams, and very hard is more than 180 milligrams.

Never wash stainless-steel cutlery or flatware together with silver or silver-plated cutlery or flatware. The two metals can react against each other and cause the silver to become pitted or stained. Keep children, especially toddlers, away from door vents. During drying they can emit steam.

Disinfectants

Uses: The purpose of disinfectants is simple: to kill germs. But from there, disinfecting can get complicated because germs—undesirable and harmful microorganisms—are amazingly varied and surprisingly clever. They're also good at what they do: reproducing, causing disease, creating foul odors, spoiling food, causing stains, and destroying fabric. In response, manufacturers have come up with a variety of products designed to disinfect.

Antibacterial cleaners: These are the most popular and common disinfectants. Most of them are formulated with quaternary ammonium compound—"quats," for short—because it combines well with dirt- and grease-fighting chemicals and is also an excellent broad-spectrum germ killer. They're good for cleaning and disinfecting large surfaces, such as floors and counters. Other uses include cleaning toilet bowls, sinks, and tubs.

Fungicides: Fungi produce mold and mildew. They're actually a kind of plant. Fungicides can wipe out these buggers before they create a mess. One of the most effective fungicides is plain old chlorine bleach. Diluted (3 tablespoons bleach with 1 quart water) and placed in a spray bottle, it will kill mildew and at the same time bleach the stain that mildew creates. Disinfectant cleaners that contain quats are another weapon against mold and mildew. They have the power to kill fungus before it grows mold or mildew. Finally, perhaps the best fungicide is adequate light and dry air since fungus thrives in damp dark places.

Germicides: This is just another way of saying "disinfectant." Products that claim to be germicides for use on hard surfaces contacted in everyday living, like countertops, refrigerators, and door handles, must also be officially registered as disinfectants with the Environmental Protection Agency (EPA), says Joseph Rubino, director of biological sciences for Reckitt and Coleman in Montvale, New Jersey, the company that makes Lysol brand products. "You can't call it a germicide if it isn't a disinfectant," he says.

How to buy: When buying a disinfectant, look for an official EPA registration number on the label. This means that the product has been properly registered as a germ-killer. The EPA defines a disinfectant as a product that kills 100 percent of the targeted germs on a surface that has already been cleaned of heavy soil. The effectiveness of most disinfectants plummets in the presence of organic matter like food, milk, hair, feces, urine, or dander. Also look for the active disinfectant ingredient—usually quaternary ammonium compound or pine oil.

Caution: Don't try to make your own disinfectants at home. Combining chemicals can be tricky. You run the risk of destroying the germ-killing effects of the chemicals. And there's also the very real danger of creating toxic or volatile mixtures. When using disinfectants, carefully read product labels for proper usage and safety precautions.

Some disinfectants can irritate your skin or eyes. As with any cleaning product, wear rubber gloves when using disinfectants, especially if you have sensitive skin. Also, remember that effective germ killing takes a little time. Leave the disinfectant in contact with the surface for a good 10 minutes, then completely rinse the chemical off with fresh water.

Dust Cloths and Dusters

Uses: The point of a dust cloth is not to just spread dust around but to capture the soil, remove it, and dispose of it. A good dusting tool should attract dust and hold it. It should also be able to reach into the cracks and crevices.

One of the best general dusting tools is a white square of cotton (flannel is excellent) spritzed with a dust remover, like Endust, so that the cloth is moist but not wet. Ideally, dust cloths should be treated, tightly covered, and stored overnight in a plastic bag before using to give the oil a chance to saturate the cloth evenly.

For dusting knickknacks and hard-to-reach places, use a lamb's wool duster. You can also buy electrostatic dust cloths, which use static electricity to attract particles and are available from janitorial supply companies.

How to buy: You can buy aerosol dust remover (like Endust) in the supermarket. It's also available from janitorial supply stores as a liquid that you put in your own spray bottle. Lamb's wool dusters hold dust better than feather dusters. Feather dusters tend to spread dust around and should be avoided. Dusters are available at home supply stores and janitorial supply stores.

Caution: Store treated dust cloths in plastic bags to avoid leaving oil stains on the surface they come in contact with.

Dustpans

Uses: Dustpans provide a handy way to pick up debris—even the fine stuff like powdery dust and cat hair—after sweeping.

How to buy: For outdoor use, look for the larger heavier models that can handle bigger loads. For indoors, the kind with a rubber lip is best because it allows you to sweep up fine dust. If you want to avoid excessive bending, consider a long-handle dustpan, which is available at janitorial supply stores.

Caution: Make sure that your dustpan is wider than the broom you plan to use with it. Otherwise, you'll sweep some particles and litter around the edge of the dustpan.

Enzyme Digesters

Uses: Enzyme digesters actually "eat" some spills. They're best for removing organic matter like urine, vomit, blood, and fecal matter from porous surfaces and objects (clothing and carpeting, for starters). You can use enzyme detergents to presoak laundry and also (when mixed up as a paste) as a spotting agent—even on dry cleanables. There are a few enzyme drain openers, which work more slowly but are safer and much less harsh on plumbing fixtures and the environment. They actually contain friendly bacteria that take up residence in your pipes and eat the goopy organic stuff that contributes to drain clogs.

How to buy: You'll find enzyme detergents and bleaches in the supermarket (Biz, for example). You can also purchase bacterial digestive enzyme products that contain proteolytic enzymes for protein stains like meat juice, egg, blood, or milk, and amylolytic enzymes for starch and carbohydrates stains. Bacterial drain cleaners, such as Rid-X Septic System Treatment, are available in supermarkets and home stores.

Caution: Don't use enzyme digestants on wool or silk. The fabric will be eaten right along with the stain. Enzyme drain treatments will help maintain free-flowing pipes, but they don't have the chemical power to clear out a badly clogged drain.

Floor Machines

Uses: These machines have two basic uses. First, floor machines clean and strip floors of soil and finish. Then, when you change from the cleaning/stripping chemicals and pad, the machine will apply a floor finish with woolly or synthetic buffing pads. In years past, the finish was usually wax. But today, floors are finished with a water-based synthetic polymer finish.

How to buy: Using a floor machine is worthwhile, but you probably need it only once a year. So it's better to rent one from your local rental store. If you want to buy, consider scoping out secondhand and thrift stores. You can often pick up one there for a song.

Caution: Floor machines are heavy electrical appliances. Follow the directions that come with the machine. Always unplug before changing pads or chemicals. Wear boots or sturdy shoes when operating.

Gloves—Rubber

Uses: Gloves to protect your hands should be a standard part of your cleaning kit, especially if you use chemicals any harsher than liquid dishwashing detergent or neutral cleaners. Rubber gloves, usually made of synthetic materials like latex, neoprene, or PVC (polyvinyl chloride), form a barrier between your skin and cleaning surfaces, tools, and chemicals, says John Becker, sales manager at Easterday Janitorial Supply Company in San Francisco, one of the West Coast's largest janitorial companies. They also allow you to withstand hotter temperatures when cleaning with hot water.

How to buy: Get a pair of gloves that are one size bigger than your hands to make it easier to get them on and off. If you're working with specialty chemicals, make sure that the glove package indicates that the material will protect against those chemicals. Look for these gloves at janitorial supply stores. Buy two pairs at the same time, suggests Bill R. Griffin, president of Cleaning Consultant Services in Seattle, which provides literature, videos, software, and seminars about cleaning.

Caution: Discard gloves with holes—even tiny ones. Liquid will enter the glove and be held against your skin by the glove.

Hair Spray

Uses: Besides holding hair in place, hair spray is a surprisingly effective spot removing agent and laundry pretreatment for ink. The effective ingredients are alcohol and volatile solvents and resins.

How to buy: "Try a men's unscented hair spray," recommends Bill R. Griffin, president of Cleaning Consultant Services in Seattle, which provides literature, videos, software, and seminars about cleaning. More expensive hair sprays often contain ingredients that will stain.

Caution: Always test on an inconspicuous place on the garment (or on similar fabric) first. Be especially careful with wool, acetate, and silk. Launder garments after using hair spray as a spot remover since it will make the fabric stiff.

Hydrogen Peroxide

Uses: A form of bleach, hydrogen peroxide works well as a spotting chemical on fabric, especially for blood and scorch marks, says Bill R. Griffin, president of Cleaning Consultant Services in Seattle, which provides literature, videos, software, and seminars about cleaning. And, of course, hydrogen peroxide can also be used as an antiseptic.

How to buy: Buy the 3 percent solution sold in drugstores. Buy only as much as you will need right away because its strength decreases when it sits for too long.

Caution: Hydrogen peroxide may be used on most fabrics, even silk, acetate, and wool, which are chlorine-sensitive. But always pretest on an inconspicuous spot first.

Laundry Pretreaters

Uses: Today's washing machines and laundry detergents are good, but they're not good enough to erase extra soils and small stains without pretreating. That's where laundry sticks, sprays, and liquid pretreatments do their work. The liquids (which, technically, include the spray and aerosol varieties) are the most effective at softening and dissolving grease and oil spots, says Bill R. Griffin, president of Cleaning Consultant Services in Seattle, which provides literature, videos, software, and seminars about cleaning. There's a drawback to the liquids, though. You should use them only 3 to 5 minutes before washing a garment. That means that the stain may have set in the fabric while it was sitting in the laundry hamper for 3 to 5 days.

That's where sticks have the advantage. Although they're not quite as powerful as the liquids, you can make up for that by treating the stain soon after it happens. Then toss the garment back into the hamper for a full laundering later. But it's still best to launder as soon as possible. Don't wait, says Griffin.

How to buy: All the pretreatments perform fairly well. You can buy both the liquids (such as Shout) and the sticks (such as Spray 'n Wash) in grocery and variety stores. Experiment with a few brands and settle on the one or two that work best for the kind of stains you and your family get into.

Caution: Avoid breathing the fumes or getting the spray on your skin or in your eyes. Always read the product label for proper use and safety precautions. Don't use laundry pretreatments on upholstery and carpet, which can't be laundered.

Lemon Juice

Uses: You thought it was just for adding some kick to your tea? As an emergency spot remover and occasional cleaning and spotting chemical, lemon juice is hard to beat. Traditionally, homemakers have used it to remove alkaline stains left by liquor, coffee, tea, and other tannins, says John Becker, sales manager at Easterday Janitorial Supply Company in San Francisco, one of the West Coast's largest janitorial companies. "Today, even professional cleaners are going back to the way Grandma used to clean—with lemon juice, vinegar, baking soda, and salt." Mixed with salt, lemon juice can do a respectable job on even tough stains like wine. As a spot remover, lemon juice, which is citric acid, can knock out stains on fabric (rub lemon juice directly onto the stain) and even on harder surfaces like laminate. (Make a poultice with baking soda and lemon juice, smear on, and let dry.)

How to buy: Simply buy fresh lemons and slice them open for the juice, or buy bottled juice made from concentrate.

Caution: Lemon juice also contains some fruit sugar, which can leave a sticky residue and even stain. It must be rinsed thoroughly after use as a cleaner or spot remover. Test first before using on silk, wool, cotton, linen, rayon, or acetate. Avoid using lemon juice to clean metals; it can tarnish them if left in contact.

Mops—Dust, Wet

Uses: Mops are the perfect solution for light cleaning of flooring. If you are faced with heavy-duty grime on a floor, you will need something tougher than a mop—usually a sturdy scrub brush or a long-handle scrubber with a nylon-pad attachment. When it comes to mopping, though, there are two issues: getting the loose dirt and dust off the floor, and removing the dried-on grime from the surface. Each of those issues involves a different type of mop.

Dust Mop

Dust mops get dust off large floors more completely and more quickly than sweeping, and they grab onto the finest particles. For best results, treat your dust mop with a dusting spray such as Endust, which makes it attract and hold particles. Shake out your dust mop and give it a light misting of dusting spray after use to restore its dust-catching power.

How to buy: Dust mops are available at home stores. The 18-inch size is convenient for the home.

Wet Mop

For most homes with relatively little flooring—just the bathrooms and the kitchen—a simple sponge mop is usually sufficient. Use it with a light-duty

HOW THE LAKERS MOP UP

You may not have to clean a floor as large as the Great Western Forum, where the Los Angeles Lakers play basketball. But you can still use the same mopping technique perfected by the professionals to make floors shine.

Louie Galicia, operations manager for the Lakers, says that this is his tried-and-true drill for perfect mopping.

1. Mop the floor with a good dust mop to remove all the loose dirt.

2. Using a separate bucket for washing and rinsing, mop the floor with a string or sponge mop. Use a mild floor detergent and change the rinse bucket whenever it looks murky.

3. When the floor is dry, go over it once again with a clean dust mop.

"We've been using this method for years and years, and it works wonders," says Galicia.

cleaner, such as a squirt of liquid dishwashing detergent in a bucket. You can also use a sponge mop for applying wax to waxable floors, but it's not ideal. A lamb's wool applicator leaves fewer bubbles in the wax. For mopping large areas of flooring, consider a string mop, which does the job faster. String mops also go into tight corners and clean under cabinets easier than sponge mops.

How to buy: You can buy sponge mops in grocery stores, discount department stores, or home stores. The type with a built-in squeeze wringer works well, but be sure to get one with sturdy hardware.

For home use, try a 16-ounce string mop. They're available at home stores and janitorial supply stores.

Caution: After use, be sure to rinse wet mops thoroughly, then allow them to hang dry by their handles to avoid mildewing.

Oils—Lemon, Linseed, Neat's-Foot, Pine, Tung

Uses: Oils extracted from animals and plants are among the most traditional of cleaners and protectants. Use the right oil for the right job.

Lemon Oil

Lemon oil has a pleasant scent. Used to beautify and preserve dry or bare wood, it can also restore the glow and depth to varnished or sealed wood, polish stainless steel, brighten the finish on laminate, protect ceramic tile from soap scum, and shine anodized aluminum.

Linseed Oil

Used mostly to help condition and seal bare wood, linseed oil is derived from the seed of flax, or linseed. It's especially good for protecting outdoor furniture from the elements. Linseed oil may not be listed on product labels, but it is an ingredient in many paints, varnishes, and stains.

Neat's-Foot Oil

If you know that "neat" is an old-fashioned word for "cattle," then you probably can guess that neat's-foot oil is derived from cattle hooves. This amber-hue oil is used mostly as a leather conditioner—on baseball gloves, saddles, and work boots—keeping the leather soft and supple. Don't use it on items that you want to shine, however, because it leaves a dull finish that is hard to polish.

Pine Oil

A natural resin distilled from pine trees, pine oil is used mostly as an ingredient in all-purpose cleaners. These products have the power to clean, deodorize, and to some degree, disinfect. Only cleaners with 20 percent or more pine oil are effective germ-fighters, though. "Unless they are very concentrated, most pine cleaners are more likely to make the germs smell better than to kill them," says Bill R. Griffin, president of Cleaning Consultant Services in Seattle, which provides literature, videos, software, and seminars about cleaning.

Tung Oil

Extracted from the nut of the tung tree, tung oil penetrates into wood pores and forms a seal against moisture. The oil dries hard but never loses its elasticity. Tung oil is often found as an ingredient in oil-based paints and varnishes, but you can also use it alone as a sealer and protective coating for wood surfaces.

How to buy: Furniture-care oils and finishes are available at hardware and home stores. Neat's-foot oil can be found at specialty shoe and luggage shops. You can buy pine oil cleaners at grocery and variety stores and at janitorial supply stores. Tung oil can be found at home stores.

Caution: Since linseed oil dries slowly, don't use furniture treated with it for a few days. Carefully dispose of cloths used to apply oil such as linseed and tung oil because they can spontaneously combust. Submerge cloths in water and place the container outside of the building. When buying pine oil cleaners, make sure that the ingredients include pine oil. Many are simply scented with pine perfume. Always read product labels for proper use and safety precautions.

Polishes and Waxes

Uses: Polishing and waxing have become less popular in more recent years as we've gotten busier with work and family and as the surfaces we used to polish and wax have gotten easier to care for. Still, if you really want to put a shine on many types of furniture, floors, or cars, you have to haul out the polish or wax and crank up the elbow grease.

Furniture

A good dusting with a dusting spray such as Endust will spruce up most wood furniture. Dusting spray will also protect the wood because dusting with a dry cloth can scratch and dull wood's finish. If the finish does become dull or scratched, waxing or polishing can certainly help.

Products such as Pledge furniture polish contain polishes and cleaners, so they clean and leave a shine behind. Don't use excessive amounts of polish, though. It attracts dust.

Older and antique furniture can benefit from old-fashioned paste wax because it fills in small cracks and scratches. It takes a long time to dry, though, and after applying, it must be buffed.

Floors

Newer vinyl no-wax and laminate floors don't require finish or wax but will benefit from an occasional coat of polish. Just wash them with a product specially made for your type of floor. But linoleum, older hardwood, and cork floors need to be stripped and rewaxed or finished periodically. Most of the "waxes" you can buy at the store today aren't waxes at all but clear polymer finishes, such as Future. These products can be used on no-wax and vinyl floors but not wood or cork. You apply them wet, and when they dry, they leave a shiny hard surface behind. Traditional wood floors that are not sealed with a hard-coat finish can be waxed with special liquid or paste wax for wood floors. Be sure that the wax doesn't include water, which can damage the floor. On wood or laminate floors, use a very well wrung out mop. Excessive moisture will damage the floor.

Car

Automobile finishes are much harder today than they were even 10 years ago, so waxing is not as crucial today. Still, a good waxing will give your car a certain sparkle, and older cars will benefit by having the layer of oxidized paint removed with wax. Today's car "waxes" are as sophisticated as the paints they're designed to clean and protect. They are made of complicated mixtures of wax, silicones, and polymers.

How to buy: Furniture polish and waxes are available at grocery and discount department stores. You'll find more specialized waxes at hardware stores. For waxing nonwood floors, look for a newer polymer finish such as Future. Do not apply any type of coating to laminate floors. For real waxing, you can get liquid wax, which is easier to apply but doesn't offer quite as much protection as paste wax. You'll find products like Future in grocery stores, discount department stores, and home stores. You'll find liquid and paste waxes at home stores. Car waxes and polishes are best purchased at an auto supply or discount department store.

Caution: Be loyal to one brand and type of furniture polish. Switching between types and brands can damage wood's finish. Always read product labels for proper use and safety precautions.

Polishing Cloths

Uses: Polishing cloths have a dual purpose: applying polish and buffing a polished surface. You can use the same cloth for both jobs by flipping or refolding the cloth to expose a fresh buffing surface. Or use two separate cloths.

How to buy: For most polishing jobs—on furniture, metal, and automobiles, for instance—you can use a square of absorbent natural fabric such as cotton flannel or cotton diaper cloth. Special polishing cloths are usually made of a cotton or feltlike material and sold for especially delicate jobs such as instrument polishing. You can also buy polishing cloths already impregnated with metal polish. Look for these in hardware stores.

Caution: Synthetic fabrics such as polyester, nylon, and rayon make poor polishing cloths. They're not absorbent enough. Avoid dyed or printed fabrics; the solvents in some polishes can cause the color to bleed onto the thing you're polishing. Also, don't use cloths with any buttons, clips, or zippers.

Poultices

Uses: A poultice is a paste used for drawing a stain out of hard surfaces such as laminate, unsealed concrete, marble, granite, and other porous stone. You can make a poultice from many different combinations of powdered or granular absorbents and liquid solvents or acids. Typical poultice recipes include baking soda and lemon juice (for stains on laminate), cat litter and paint thinner (for stains on concrete), and chalk or talc with paint thinner or lighter fluid (for stains on porous stone). You place the pastelike mixture on the stain, sometimes more than once, and allow it to dry. Then sweep, wipe, or vacuum it away.

How to buy: Most of the ingredients of poultices—such as cat litter, baking soda, chalk, lighter fluid, paint thinner, and lemon juice—are available at grocery stores, discount department stores, and home stores. You can also buy commercially prepared poultices from specialty stone-care dealers.

Caution: Be sure to test poultices first on an inconspicuous spot before applying them to stains. If you make a poultice from a volatile solvent, be sure to use it in a well-ventilated area. Also, cover solvent-based poultices for a while with a damp cloth or plastic wrap to keep them from drying out too soon. Always read product labels for proper use and safety precautions.

Pumice

Uses: Pumice stone, which is made from the hardened foam of volcanic lava, is used mostly as an abrasive. It has just the right hardness to scratch off stains and hardened soils from brick, cast-iron cookware, concrete, cooking grills, and toilet bowls.

How to buy: You'll find inexpensive pumice stone at hardware and janitorial supply stores.

Caution: Be sure to use pumice stones wet to protect the surface being scoured. The abrasiveness that makes pumice good for scrubbing hard durable surfaces makes it dangerous on softer materials. Don't use it on laminate, cultured marble, enameled metals, plastics, or fiberglass. If you use it in combination with acid when cleaning a toilet bowl, wear rubber gloves.

Razor Blades

Uses: Razor blades are excellent for light scraping, especially for taking dried paint, candle wax, and stickers off glass and mirrors.

How to buy: Always get the single-edge blades designed to fit in a retractable safety holder. You'll find these at hardware and home stores. For covering large areas, you can buy 3- or 4-inch blades and holders at a janitorial supply store.

Caution: Obviously, razor blades are extremely dangerous because of their sharpness. When removing paint or stickers from glass, wet the surface, keep your fingers clear, and push a single-edge razor blade under the substance to be removed. Replace blades often; dull blades are unsafe and may scratch the surface. Be cautious using razor blades in extremely cold temperatures—they can become brittle and break. Never use a razor blade to scrape on softer materials like Plexiglas, wood, vinyl, or plastic. It will scratch and even puncture the surface.

Rubbing Compound

Uses: Rubbing compound is used to gently abrade a surface, remove scratches and oxidation, and leave a smooth surface. You can use it to get rid of small scratches on Plexiglas, cultured marble, and fiberglass. Jeweler's rouge or plastic compound would do the job even better, says Bill R. Griffin, president of Cleaning Consultant Services in Seattle, which provides literature, videos, software, and seminars about cleaning.

How to buy: Rubbing compound is available in hardware, discount, and automotive stores. Jeweler's rouge and plastic compound are available through jeweler supply and lapidary supply stores.

Caution: Like all abrasives, rubbing compound does its work by removing a thin layer of the surface being cleaned, so be cautious not to use it excessively or on surfaces with a thin veneer of paint. Test an obscure spot first. Don't rub any harder or longer than necessary or bear down too hard. Rinse frequently to assess your progress. Automotive paint experts do not recommended using rubbing compound, especially on newer clear-coat paints. Since rubbing compounds remove the critical ultraviolet protection layer of these paints, repeated use can cause the paint to prematurely deteriorate, says Michael J. Horvath, an automotive technology expert in Allentown, Pennsylvania.

Scouring Powders

Uses: The tough-guy scouring powders of old contained silicate (that is, sand) that could be really hard on surfaces like toilet bowls and bathtubs. Today's scouring powders are much milder. You can use them safely to clean basins, tubs and tiles, matte-finish stainless steel, and baked enamel cookware. You can also use a mixture of scouring powder and water to make a poultice for lifting stains off some hard surfaces.

How to buy: Available in grocery and discount department stores, these products are fairly similar. Some contain bleach.

Caution: Scouring powders can scratch many surfaces. Don't mix scouring powder that contains bleach with other cleaning chemicals, especially those with ammonia. Dangerous fumes can result. Always read product labels for proper use and safety precautions.

Sealants

Uses: Sealants are used as a barrier between the world of dirt and grime and a broad range of absorbent or permeable materials, like carpet, upholstery, and concrete. The basic strategy is to block soil from penetrating and being absorbed. Sealed textiles and surfaces are thus easier to clean and keep clean.

How to buy: For textiles, look for a fluorocarbon-type stain repellent such as Scotchgard, available in home and hardware stores. Aerosol sprayers (as opposed to pump sprayers) deliver the most consistent coating. Professional cleaning services can also apply sealants and stain repellents. Protective sealers for wood and masonry are available in home and hardware stores.

Caution: Silicone sealants for fabrics and carpets protect only against water-based stains (not oil-based) and can yellow with exposure to sunlight. Avoid using these products, advises Bill R. Griffin, president of Cleaning Consultant Services in Seattle, which provides literature, videos, software, and seminars about cleaning. Use Teflon- or fluorocarbon-based products. Always read product labels for proper use and safety precautions.

Soap

Uses: Real soap—the stuff made from fats and oils brought into chemical contact with alkalies—is commonly used for bath bars and laundry products like Ivory Snow. Soap gently cleans by lowering the surface tension of water (just like surfactants in a detergent) and by emulsifying oils and fats so that they can be rinsed away.

How to buy: Buy soaps at grocery stores, discount department stores, and drugstores.

Caution: Unlike detergents, soap combines with the minerals in hard water and can form a bathtub ring.

Solvents

Uses: Chemical solvents, which are derived from plant or petroleum products, have the wondrous ability to dissolve stains and soils. They're also used to thin paint and varnish. Here's a primer.

Acetone: One of the most powerful solvents, acetone is made from alcohol. It can be diluted with water and used to remove nail polish, airplane glue, rubber cement, and grease.

Alcohol: Use denatured or isopropyl alcohol to remove grease and grime from metal objects and glass and as a spot remover for grass stains, inks, and dyes.

Amyl acetate: Amyl acetate is hard to find, but it can do most of the things that acetone does. And it's safe on acetate and other fabrics that are destroyed by acetone.

Mineral spirits: Alias paint thinner, this petroleum distillate is effective for removing lots of oil and grease stains from machine parts, metal, concrete, and hard plastic surfaces. It's good for cleaning up oil-based paint spatters and paintbrushes and rollers used for oil painting. It's found in commercial preparations to remove adhesives and paints.

Turpentine: Distilled from the sap of pine trees, turpentine is an excellent thinner of oil paints, but it's not great for cleaning and degreasing because it leaves a sticky residue.

How to buy: Buy turpentine and mineral spirits at home, hardware, and paint stores. You can find acetone and alcohol at hardware stores, grocery stores, or drugstores. D-limonene, a citrus-based solvent, is considered an organic replacement for petroleum-based solvents. Look for products such as Citrus Strip, which contains d-limonene, in home, hardware, and paint stores.

Caution: Though effective, solvents are often flammable, usually toxic, and also hard on the environment. They can be absorbed through the skin and through breathing the fumes. Some solvents are harmful to silk, acetate, wool, and nylon; they dissolve the fabric. When using solvents, wear gloves and make sure that the area is well-ventilated. Always read product labels for proper use and safety precautions.

Sponges

Uses: Sponges are efficient for cleaning and wiping smooth surfaces, from dinner plates to plate glass to walls. They drip less and hold more cleaning solution and soil than cloths or paper towels. Don't use sponges where bacteria control or food safety are issues, advises Bill R. Griffin, pres-

THE DIRTY LITTLE SECRET OF SPONGES

You think of sponges as a cleaning tool, right? But they can easily turn into germ dispensers, smearing nasty microbes all over your kitchen countertops, cabinets, refrigerator handles, and more. The problem is that continually moist cellulose sponges provide just the right environment for colony-forming microbes— a surface to cling to, moisture, and a steady supply of nutrients. The same holds true for cotton dishcloths.

"If there's ever a new life form on the planet, it's going to come from the sponge. There are billions and billions of microbes on them," says Charles Gerba, Ph.D., professor of microbiology at the University of Arizona in Tucson, who conducted a study of 75 dishcloths and 325 sponges from home kitchens and found large numbers of virulent bacteria, including *Escherichia coli* and strains of *Salmonella, Pseudomonas,* and *Staphylococcus.*

The good news is that there's an easy way to sterilize your sponge: Let your dishwasher do the work. You can disinfect sponges in your dishwasher at the same time as you clean your glassware, dishes, and flatware.

You can also sanitize a sponge with household bleach, says Gayle Coleman, R.D., a food, nutrition, and health education associate program leader with the Michigan State University Extension in East Lansing. The Clorox Company recommends mixing ¾ cup bleach in 1 gallon water and soaking your sponges in the solution for 5 minutes to kill germs. There is no need to rinse.

ident of Cleaning Consultant Services in Seattle, which provides literature, videos, software, and seminars about cleaning.

How to buy: You can get cellulose sponges at supermarkets, drugstores, and home stores. Natural sponges are harder to find. If you buy the type of cellulose sponge with abrasive backing, make sure that you get one with the correct level of abrasion for the job (white pads are the least abrasive; blue is a bit more abrasive; green is medium; and black is the scratchiest of all). Use the sponges with the white abrasive backing for your household chores, says Griffin. The others will damage almost any surface.

Caution: Make sure that you clean your sponge with mild liquid dishwashing detergent after use, then allow it to dry so that bacteria don't multiply. Because you can't get inside your sponge to sterilize it, Griffin recommends using the antibacterial variety available at most supermarkets. Replace your sponge once a month.

Spot Removers

Uses: Spot removers designed for general use on fabric or carpet come in two varieties: wet and "dry." The wet spotters, such as Whink Instant Spot Remover (for clothes) or Whink Carpet Stain Remover (for upholstery and carpets), are made to get out spots made by such things as cola, fruit juice, and coffee. They are formulated from water-based detergents. The dry spotters, such as Carbona Stain Devils and K2r, are made from solvents and are effective against grease, oil, tar, and other solvent-soluble messes.

How to buy: Spot removers are available in supermarkets, hardware stores, home stores, or discount department stores on the carpet-cleaning shelf. Look for brands such as Afta, Carbona Stain Devils, Energine, K2r, Renuzite, and Thoro. You can also buy industrial brands (usually at lower cost) at a janitorial supply store.

Caution: Depending on the kind of stain, a spill may require specialty chemicals or even professional care. Solvent-based spot removers are flammable and require adequate ventilation. Also, use solvent-based spot removers in small amounts on upholstery and carpet because solvents deteriorate foam, latex adhesives, and carpet glue. Always read product labels for proper use and safety precautions.

Squeegees

Uses: Using a squeegee is the fastest, most efficient way to clean a window or mirror. You can also keep a squeegee handy in the bathroom to

THE SQUEEGEE: GIVE YOUR WINDOWS A SHAVE

Glass-cleaning solution loosens dirt and floats it off the window. The squeegee then dries the window by shaving the dirty water off the surface. But the more solution you put on, the more you have to shave off, so use a damp window scrubber, not one that is dripping wet.

When you scrub a window with paper towels, balled-up newspaper, or a cloth, dirt is wiped around the window and cleaned up a little at a time instead of being lifted off with a few quick strokes.

quickly wipe down a shower stall after use and thus prevent mildew formation and soap scum buildup.

How to buy: Squeegees are available at home stores. The best-quality squeegees are sold by janitorial supply stores. For home use, the 12-inch size is the easiest to manage, says Margaret Dasso, owner of the Clean Sweep, a professional cleaning service based in Lafayette, California, and coauthor of *Dirt Busters*. If you plan to use your squeegee a lot, don't buy one with a built-in applicator sponge. Once the sponge wears out, you'll have to buy a whole new squeegee.

Caution: Don't wipe the blade with a dry cloth when using—it won't slide over the glass surface as easily. Use a damp cloth instead. When the blade wears out, replace it if possible (you can do that with the better squeegees), or toss the squeegee and buy a new one.

Steam Cleaners

Uses: Steam-cleaning is one of the most effective ways to deep clean carpet. Also called hot-water extraction, it involves a machine that sprays a blast of heated cleaning detergent into the carpet, which loosens dirt and is then sucked up with a strong vacuum. This method is excellent for removing the tons of dirt and grime that accumulate in your carpet pile over the years.

How to buy: You can rent—or even buy—hot-water extraction equipment at rental supplies and sometimes at supermarkets. But consumer and rental machines are not nearly as effective as the machines used by professional carpet cleaners, and they tend to overwet the carpet, says Bill R. Griffin, president of Cleaning Consultant Services in Seattle, which provides literature, videos, software, and seminars about cleaning. The best approach is to use a professional who is certified by the Institute of Inspection, Cleaning, and Restoration Certification (IICRC). To find a certified professional in your area, write to the IICRC at 2715 East Mill Plain Boulevard, Vancouver, WA 98661. Include your ZIP code and they'll send you the names of several professionals in your area.

Steel Wool

Uses: One of the toughest nonchemical cleaning tools, steel wool works as an abrasive to remove stubborn stains and gunk. But because it's so harsh, steel wool is generally reserved for times when other methods have failed, and even then you should only use it on surfaces that are very hard or that you don't mind scratching. It works well for scrubbing burnt-on grease from broiling pans and is also effective at removing crud from cast-iron cookware. The very finest grades of steel wool can be used for delicate cleaning tasks, such as removing rust spots from polished metals and wood before repolishing. It's also an excellent way to sand surfaces between coats of paint or varnish.

How to buy: Steel wool is available in home and hardware stores in grades ranging from #0000 (superfine) to #4 (extra-coarse). You can also find steel wool impregnated with soap at supermarkets and hardware stores.

Caution: Steel wool will scratch other metals (including gold, brass, copper, and silver) as well as wood, plastic, paint, fiberglass, and laminate.

Steel wool with the grade of #0000 will not scratch, if used cautiously. This grade will remove hard-water stains and pits from chrome, says Bill R. Griffin, president of Cleaning Consultant Services in Seattle, which provides literature, videos, software, and seminars about cleaning. Use a white scrubbing pad for other surfaces.

Toothpaste

Uses: Because it's a mild abrasive, toothpaste can clean more than teeth. It can be used to gently scrub intricate engraved metal and, mixed with water, will polish away water rings or white marks on wood furniture. It also can be used to clean the grout between ceramic tiles in the shower.

How to buy: Get the plain white paste. Colored toothpastes can leave stains of their own.

Caution: Just like other abrasives, toothpaste can scratch and dull softer surfaces, especially when rubbed too hard. It's best to test on a small inconspicuous area first. Thin the toothpaste with water. Try baking soda first.

Vacuum Cleaners

Uses: The role of a vacuum cleaner goes right to the heart of the cleaning enterprise: to pick up soil, encase it, and dispose of it. Different types of vacuums have been developed to specialize in certain cleaning situations. Here's a rundown.

Uprights: The most popular type of vacuum, uprights excel at cleaning carpets. With their beater bars and powerful suction, uprights first loosen, then extract the dust and dirt that otherwise would provide enough grit and abrasion to scratch the fibers over time. Most uprights have borrowed some ideas from canister vacuums and come with hoses and attachments that can be used to sweep and suction bare floors and other surfaces.

Canister: Usually more powerful and handier for cleaning stairs, upholstery, and hard-to-reach spots, a canister does its best work on bare floors. Many canisters have borrowed a page from the upright book and come with a power nozzle that will do a respectable job sucking debris from carpet.

Wet-dry: Wet-dry vacuums can pick up dry waste and liquid messes, too. They're handy to have around if your basement floods, or for cleaning up after construction or floor stripping. A 1-gallon wet vacuum is available for quick and easy spot or soil removal.

How to buy: Buying a vacuum can be a complicated undertaking. Look for a reputable dealer, and research consumer information before jumping in. Look for an easy-to-operate on-off switch and a model that allows you to adjust the cleaning height. The cord should be easy to pull out and rewind, and the bag should be easy to replace. Check its weight—and imagine yourself lugging it up and down stairs. Check whether the noise it makes is acceptable.

When you go to try out vacuum cleaners, take along some debris that represents the typical cleaning situations in your home—like pet hair, sand, or cracker crumbs. Also "test-drive" your prospective vacuum cleaner on both carpet and a hard surface, and to see how well it gets into corners and under furniture. Note how wide an area the vacuum cleans. Sure, the bigger the swath, the fewer the strokes. But there's a trade-off: A larger swath means reduced suction and, therefore, less cleaning power. Bill R. Griffin, president of Cleaning Consultant Services in Seattle, which provides literature, videos, software, and seminars about cleaning, recommends a swath of 12 inches or less. Also, when you're shopping for a vacuum, ask the salesperson about each unit's power to move air (expressed as cubic feet per minute, or cfm). A higher cfm means more air movement and better cleaning.

Heavy-duty vacuums, which have sturdier engines and moving parts, are available in janitorial supply stores.

Caution: As a vacuum bag fills, its suction efficiency is drastically reduced. Recent changes in bags allow them to filter smaller soil particles out of the air. These may pack the bag and decrease air movement. Pat the paper bag occasionally to knock soil out and increase air movement through the bag, suggests Griffin. Items that get caught in a vacuum's brush or fan blades may cause the motor to overheat and burn out. Many machines have an automatic shutoff for these situations, but monitor the vacuum and try to turn it off as quickly as possible.

Vinegar

Uses: Also known as acetic acid, vinegar is a cheap and useful household cleaner and spot remover. As a cleaner, it's most effective in counteracting alkaline residue. Use it (½ cup white vinegar per gallon of water) to rinse the alkaline residue left behind by wax strippers and floor cleaners, says Bill R. Griffin, president of Cleaning Consultant Services in Seattle, which provides literature, videos, software, and seminars about cleaning. You can also add it to the rinse water when doing dishes by hand. Use about 1 ounce vinegar in a full sink of water, says Griffin. That helps neutralize and rinse away detergent residue and leaves behind shiny, less-spotted glassware. Wear rubber gloves when rinsing with vinegar, warns Griffin. The acid in it can dry out your skin and fingernails. Straight vinegar also works as a lime deposit remover in coffeemakers, coffeepots, and teapots. Vinegar acts as an acid spotter, neutralizing agent, and mild bleach. Vinegar can be used on stains caused by beer, mustard, and many other common spills.

How to buy: Buy plain white distilled vinegar at the grocery store. Wine vinegar, cider vinegar, and others with plant pigment can cause stains of their own.

Caution: You can use vinegar in a pinch to do some basic cleaning chores like window washing and general cleaning. It's not as effective as a mild detergent, though, because most soils are acid, and vinegar—being an acid—will not neutralize them. As a spotting agent, vinegar shouldn't be used on cotton, linen, or acetate. It can damage the fabric. And always test it on an inconspicuous spot before using it on colored fabrics.

Index

Underscored page references indicate boxed text.